TWO VATOS TALK POP CULTURA

Latinx Pop Culture

SERIES EDITORS

Frederick Luis Aldama and Arturo J. Aldama

TWO VATOS TALK POP CULTURA

Latinx TV, Film, and Futures Unscripted

Frederick Luis Aldama and Peter Murrieta

THE UNIVERSITY OF ARIZONA PRESS
TUCSON

The University of Arizona Press
www.uapress.arizona.edu

We respectfully acknowledge the University of Arizona is on the land and territories of Indigenous peoples. Today, Arizona is home to twenty-two federally recognized tribes, with Tucson being home to the O'odham and the Yaqui. The university strives to build sustainable relationships with sovereign Native Nations and Indigenous communities through education offerings, partnerships, and community service.

ISBN-13: 978-0-8165-5772-1 (paperback)
ISBN-13: 978-0-8165-5773-8 (ebook)

Cover design by Leigh McDonald
Cover art by Miguel Angel Hernández Cedillo
Typeset by Sara Thaxton in 10.5/13.5 Warnock Pro with Futura Std

Library of Congress Cataloging-in-Publication Data are available at the Library of Congress.

Printed in the United States of America
♾ This paper meets the requirements of ANSI/NISO Z39.48-1992 (Permanence of Paper).

To my daughter and my students—breaking molds, transforming lives, and creating bold new storyworlds.
—Frederick Luis Aldama

To my children, my wife, and my students—change the world one moment and one step at a time.
—Peter Murrieta

CONTENTS

TWO VATOS TALK POP CULTURA

INTRODUCTION

Two Vatos Walk into a Cultural Revolution

We are two vatos who have spent our lives wrestling with the same protean beast—an ever-shifting media-industrial complex that constructs, packages, and disseminates the stories that define Latinx identity in the United States. One of us (Frederick) has spent a career inside the ivory tower, dissecting this media apparatus with the tools of cultural theory, semiotics, and decolonial critique. The other (Peter) has grappled with it in the writers' room, behind the camera, and at pitch meetings—trying to sneak truth past the gatekeepers of an industry that often doesn't know what to do with us.

What began as the *Mighty Peter and Professor Latinx* podcast during the COVID-19 pandemic has, after several years of further dialogue, research, and writing, morphed into this book: part cultural analysis, part creative war story, part blueprint for decolonizing the televisual and silver screens.

The Numbers Game We're Forced to Play

Let's start with what we already know but must still say aloud: Latinx communities comprise nearly 19 percent of the U.S. population and are among the most avid media consumers—yet we remain woefully underrepresented, accounting for just 2 to 6 percent of lead roles and creatives across TV and film. And when we do appear, it's often in tropes so exhausted—gangbangers, maids, spicy Latinas—they feel like a cruel joke masquerading as inclusion.

Frederick remembers sitting in a Berkeley, California, movie theater in 1997, watching *Selena* with a packed audience of brown faces. The collective gasp when Jennifer Lopez appeared in that iconic purple jumpsuit wasn't just about fashion—it was about seeing ourselves reflected with dignity, complexity, and star power. Twenty-five years later, that film still hasn't made it into the National Film Registry, despite Congressman Joaquin Castro's petitions. The message is clear: Our stories can make money, but they can't make history.

Meanwhile, Peter's experience in the writers' room tells a parallel story. During the development of *Wizards of Waverly Place* (2007–2012), he watched as network executives questioned whether a show centered on a Latina teenager could appeal to "mainstream" (read: white) audiences. The show's massive success, launching Selena Gomez's career and becoming one of Disney Channel's highest-rated series, proved what we already knew: Authentic stories resonate across communities. Yet even today, Peter regularly hears variations of the same concern: "But will it play well to viewers in Kansas, St. Louis, or Peoria?"

Infrastructures of Imagination

But this book does more than lament a lack of visibility. It's about interrogating the structural reasons behind that absence and celebrating the insurgent creativity that flourishes in the margins. The goal isn't mere inclusion in preexisting systems but a radical reimagining of what those systems could become.

We're not here to clap every time a brown face appears on screen. That's table scraps disguised as equity. Instead, we interrogate how narratives are greenlit, who controls production pipelines, and how cultural power operates beneath surface-level diversity. We move beyond the binary of "good" versus "bad" representation to explore what scholars of race and media variously identify as the illusion of inclusion in which representational visibility is decoupled from actual structural power.

From Frederick's vantage in the academy, we stand in dialogue with foundational theorists such as Stuart Hall, whose notion of encoding/decoding reminds us that media meaning is always contested, and Raymond Williams, who defined culture as "a whole way of life" shaped by and shaping historical forces. We also draw on the Latin American intellectual tradition—Fernando Ortiz's concept of transculturation and Néstor García Canclini's hybridity—to analyze how Latinx identities are not fixed but forged in collision and fusion.

Similarly, Peter's trajectory through the TV industry, from scripting Disney's *Wizards of Waverly Place* to executive producing *Mr. Iglesias* (2019–2020) and *Primo* (2023), reveals how behind-the-scenes cultural negotiations shape what ends up on screen. Good intentions alone can't survive the development pipeline, where Latinx creatives are asked to dilute, translate, or "universalize" their stories for a white imaginary. These industrial logics check the diversity box without cultural or narrative depth or complexity.

Digital Disruptions and Battles for Narrative Space

The Latinx cultural imaginary has found new life in digital spaces that bypass traditional gatekeepers entirely. Frederick watches his students create Instagram Reels and TikTok smartphone stories that remix telenovela tropes with social justice messaging, reaching millions without ever entering a pitch meeting. Peter observes how young creators use YouTube to build audiences that rival those of cable networks, proving that hunger for authentic Latinx content far exceeds what traditional media provides.

These digital natives aren't waiting for permission. They're creating what Latinx media scholars talk about, building on the work of Walter Mignolo and Rolando Vásquez, as decolonial aesthetics in practice: content that doesn't translate itself for white audiences but instead invites viewers into fully realized Latinx worlds. When creators like Jenny Lorenzo or Los Dos Carnales go viral, they're not just entertaining—they're building alternative infrastructure for cultural production.

The rise of streaming platforms has created both opportunities and new forms of erasure. On one hand, shows like *One Day at a Time* (2017–2020), *Gentefied* (2020–2021), and *Los Espookys* (2019–2022) found homes on platforms hungry for content. On the other hand, the algorithmic logic of streaming often buries Latinx content in subcategories, making it invisible to broader audiences while simultaneously using it to claim diversity credentials.

Frederick's research into streaming metrics reveals a troubling pattern: Latinx shows are held to higher performance standards than their white counterparts, expected to deliver massive numbers imme-

Figure 1 Bernardo Velasco, Ana Fabrega, and Julio Torres star in HBO's *Los Espookys* (2019–2022) as horror-loving friends Renaldo, Tati, and Andrés.

diately or face cancellation—the fate of all three of the shows just mentioned. Meanwhile, Peter's experience shopping projects to streamers reveals another dynamic: The pressure to make Latinx stories "universal" (code for "white friendly") remains as strong as ever, just couched in the language of "global appeal."

Why?

This book emerges from a shared conviction: Latinx media representation is more than an aesthetic concern—it is urgent cultural and political work. As we write this, we're witnessing both unprecedented visibility and familiar erasures. *Blue Beetle* (2023) became the first Latinx-led superhero film in the DC Extended Universe, yet it was given a smaller marketing budget than its white-led counterparts. *In the Heights* (2021) brought Lin-Manuel Miranda's vision to screens nationwide but sparked debates about colorism and authentic representation within Latinx communities. In 2025 Bad Bunny became Spotify's most-streamed artist globally while English-language media still struggles to cover reggaeton as more than a curiosity. As we began to wrap up the book, we celebrated Zoe Saldaña's Academy Award for Best Supporting Actress in *Emilia Pérez* (2024) and *The Casagrandes Movie* (2024), which, with our friend Lalo Alcaraz at the writing table, drew deeply and respectfully from Indigenous Michoacán (Purépecha) culture. Yet we also saw plenty of Latinx shows canceled. Completed films like *Batgirl* (2022) with Dominicana Latina Leslie Grace Martínez (known for her role as Nina Rosario in *In the Heights*) were left on a postproduction editing room floor.

During this recent period, we witnessed the meteoric rise of Bad Bunny, not just as a Latinx musician recognized around the world (today he's one of the most streamed artists globally) but also as an actor in high-profile films and TV shows. But when the National Football League announced him as the 2026 Super Bowl halftime headliner, conservative backlash erupted. Many complained that he would be performing in Spanish and questioned his U.S. citizenship status—even though he's Puerto Rican and thus born with automatic U.S. citizenship. The Trump administration's then Department of Homeland Security Secretary Kristi Noem's announcement on national media that ICE would be "all over" the Super Bowl 2026 only intensified these tensions.

We write from this moment of expansion and contraction, a moment of contradiction where we see streaming platforms desperate for content yet resistant to greenlighting Latinx shows; audiences hungry for authentic stories yet served recycled stereotypes; and young Latinx creators building massive followings yet shut out of traditional development pipelines. This book maps these tensions while pointing toward possibilities.

Our collaboration models the kind of cross-pollination we advocate for in the industry. Frederick brings frameworks from cultural studies, critical race theory, and decolonial thought. Peter brings war stories from writers' rooms, insights from pitch meetings, and the practical knowledge of what it takes to get a show from concept to screen. Together, we create a kind of borderlands epistemology—knowledge produced in the spaces between academy and industry, theory and practice, critique and creation.

We don't always agree. Frederick sometimes finds Peter too willing to compromise with industry demands. Peter sometimes finds Frederick too removed from the brutal realities of keeping a show on the air. But this productive friction generates insights neither of us could reach on our own. It mirrors the larger tensions facing Latinx creators: how to maintain cultural integrity while reaching broad audiences, how to tell specific stories that resonate universally, and how to work within systems while working to transform them.

Our journey through Latinx media landscapes begins with the superhero-industrial complex (chapter 1), where we analyze how the dominant white-optic framing of superhero narratives often mishandles, distorts, or appropriates Latinx identities—superpowered or not. In chapter 2, we examine the disconnect between ideal and real audiences, questioning who is imagined as the default viewer and how that assumption shapes creative choices.

We dive deep into genre territories: the neo-Western and narco narratives that trap Latinx characters in cycles of violence (chapter 3), the sci-fi landscapes where we appear as metaphors more than people (chapter 4), and we explore how *The Mandalorian* (2019–2023) provided refuge for us during the pandemic as well as how it reconfigured Western and colonial exoticist myths (chapter 5). We then wind down with discussion and analysis of teen shows that shape young Latinx viewers' sense of possibility (chapter 6).

Our wrap-up chapters celebrate the shows and films we love and consider to have defined brown-optic-shaped Latinx narratives—not through top-down canonization but through community embrace. We conclude with a vision for the future: what Latinx media could become if freed from the constraints of mainstream (white) producer approval and its respective profit-generating motives, market fears, and anxieties.

What follows is not a manifesto but a conversation. Between a scholar-creative and a showrunner-scholar. Between critique and creation. Between borderlands and backlots. We invite you to join this dialogue and bring your own tools—whether they're syllabi, scripts, Instagram Reels, TikToks, or taglines. Because the future of Latinx media won't be made by any one vato, *profesora*, or influencer. It will be a collective endeavor forged in resistance, remix, and radical joy. As we've learned from our distinct but intertwined paths, transformation happens when we stop asking for permission and start building our own stages.

The beast we're wrestling—that white-optic media-industrial complex that has constrained and stereotyped us for generations—is powerful but not invincible. Every authentic story that makes it to screen, every comic book that centers brown heroes, every viral video that celebrates rather than translates our cultures weakens its grip. Every young creator who sees themselves reflected with complexity and dignity grows up knowing they don't need to shrink themselves to fit someone else's frame.

Let's get to work.

Chapter 1

DIVERSITY, EQUITY, AND INCLUSION IN THE ERA OF BLOCKBUSTER SUPERHEROES

Frederick still remembers that cold February Friday, the late-night showing of *Black Panther* (2018) in Columbus, Ohio. The AMC theater overflowed with Black moviegoers dressed in *Black Panther* costumes and T-shirts; some sported hybrid combos: *Black Panther* T-shirts with dashikis and/or kente-cloth scarves. The energy was electric, celebratory, almost sacred. This wasn't just another superhero movie. It was a cultural moment. As the credits rolled, Frederick thought: When will we get our Latinx superhero moment?

On the other side of the country, Peter watched *Black Panther* in a Burbank screening room, surrounded by industry colleagues who kept stealing glances at him—the lone Latino creative in a room of decision-makers suddenly aware that "diversity sells." The postscreening chatter was revealing: "We need our *Black Panther*," one executive said, meaning a Latinx superhero film. But as Peter knew from years in the business, "we need our X" usually translates to "we need a safe, sanitized version that won't challenge anyone too much."

These two viewing experiences—one communal and celebratory, the other industrial and calculating—capture the promise and limitations of diversity, equity, and inclusion (DEI) efforts in the Marvel Cinematic Universe (MCU) era. The MCU has become the dominant narrative framework of our time, grossing over $29 billion worldwide and fundamentally reshaping how stories are told, marketed, and consumed. Yet for all its cultural power, the MCU's approach to Latinx representation remains trapped between genuine attempts at inclusion and the gravitational pull of white-optic storytelling.

Frederick's experience reflects this tension. In his interview with Anthony Mackie during the 2021 release of *The Falcon and the Winter Soldier*, Mackie spoke of the miniseries as if it had aired yesterday. Mackie offered more than the usual actor's insight—he spoke from a deeply lived, Black working-class consciousness, echoing the tradition of James Baldwin. He described his return to Louisiana not just

Figure 2 In *The Falcon and the Winter Soldier* (2021), during a pivotal therapy session scene, Sam Wilson (Anthony Mackie) and Bucky Barnes (Sebastian Stan) showcase masculine emotional vulnerability rarely seen in superhero media.

as a personal homecoming, but as a deliberate act of grounding himself outside the spectacle machine of Hollywood. That return, Frederick reflects, echoes bell hooks's sense of marginal space as something one reclaims, holds onto even, because it sustains both survival and the capacity to resist.

And this resistance is not performative—it's deeply embedded in *The Falcon and the Winter Soldier*'s affective architecture. The show uses streaming's serialized form to afford emotional breadth impossible in a two-hour film. The therapy scenes between Sam Wilson and Bucky Barnes do more than advance the plot; they model masculine vulnerability rarely seen in superhero media. When Sam and Bucky repair the family boat in Louisiana, we see heroism redefined as community care, as keeping family legacy afloat—literally and metaphorically.

The series' most powerful moment comes not in an action sequence but in a banking office. Sam Wilson, who helped save the universe, can't get a loan to save his family's business. The banker, a white man who takes selfies with The Falcon, denies the loan with bureaucratic efficiency. This scene does what the best speculative fiction does: uses the fantastic to illuminate the real. Here, the supersuit can't protect against structural racism. The shield can't deflect redlining—the discriminatory practice of denying loans and services to Black and Latinx neighborhoods that continues to this day.

Frederick teaches this scene in his Comic Book Media & Identities course at the University of Texas at Austin, using *The Falcon and the Winter Soldier* to illustrate the kind of extreme discrimination Sam faces as a Black man from the South. No matter how superheroic he is (a veteran and The Falcon), this doesn't translate to economic access. Students—especially Latinx students—immediately connect this to their own experiences: the auntie who runs a successful food truck in East Austin but can't get a business loan to continue growing, the *tío* in nearby San Antonio whose nursing expertise is questioned because of his accent.

For Peter, this scene crystallizes the moment when true superpowers come into play. Patience, restraint, and the knowledge that you may be an expert, or qualified, or ready, but that doesn't mean those around you think you are. Ever proving, ever probing, we must fight on in all ways, including holding our ground silently and existing being the victory on some occasions.

This understanding shapes *The Falcon and the Winter Soldier*'s introduction of Isaiah Bradley (Carl Winston Lumbly), which rewrites Captain America's origin story as a horror tale. A Black supersoldier who served his country only to be imprisoned and experimented on for thirty years, Isaiah embodies what Saidiya Hartman calls "the afterlife of slavery"—the ways anti-Black violence continues to structure American life. His grandson Eli's rage at Sam for even considering taking up the shield reflects real generational tensions within communities of color about assimilation versus resistance.

Peter recognizes these tensions from writers' rooms, where Latinx creators debate how much to explain, how much to translate, how much to make palatable. During *Mr. Iglesias*'s development, network executives pushed for the titular character to be more "aspirational," code for distancing him from working-class Latinx culture. The compromise—turning him into a successful comedian who returns to teach—maintained cultural specificity while satisfying the network's desire for positive representation.

But what does positive representation mean when the structures themselves remain unchanged? Sam Wilson becomes Captain Amer-

Figure 3 In *Mr. Iglesias* (2019–2020), the namesake history teacher (Gabriel "Fluffy" Iglesias) takes on teaching a group of gifted but misfit children to try to unlock their full potential.

ica, but the country he represents continues to marginalize Black and brown communities. The series gestures toward this contradiction in Sam's climactic speech about doing better. Standing before a crowd of politicians and cameras, he declares: "I'm a Black man, carrying the stars and stripes. What don't I understand? Every time I pick this thing up, I know there are millions of people out there who are going to hate me for it. Even now, here. I feel it. The stares, the judgment, and there's nothing I can do to change it. And I'm still here. No super serum. No blonde hair or blue eyes. The only power I have is that I believe we can do better." Sam's speech drives home the fact that racism continues to be a permanent feature of U.S. American life—one that can only ever be managed, never systematically eliminated.

Paradox of In-Visibilities

Following our critique of the white-optic dominance in superhero narratives, it's important to turn to how inclusion initiatives manifest in the biggest cultural juggernaut of our time: the MCU. While Black characters—most notably *Black Panther*, Riri Williams, and Monica Rambeau—have begun to occupy central and complex roles, Latinx characters remain frustratingly peripheral, often reduced to narrative sidebars or comic relief.

Take Joaquin Torres in *The Falcon and the Winter Soldier* and *Captain America: Brave New World* (2025). Though he hints at his comic book destiny as the next Falcon, Torres (Danny Ramirez) functions more as Sam Wilson's military sidekick than as a fully realized character. He exists in a kind of perpetual potential space: on the bench, so to speak, just visible enough to tick the representation box, but far from the playing field.

This pattern repeats across the MCU. Luis in *Ant-Man* (2015) provides comic relief through his storytelling style, which the film presents as charmingly chaotic rather than recognizing it as a sophisticated narrative tradition rooted in oral culture. Michael Peña brings depth to the role, but the writing traps him in what Charles Ramírez Berg identifies as the "male buffoon" stereotype—the Latinx character whose humor deflects from his full humanity.

Even when Latinx actors headline major roles, their ethnicity is often obscured. In the miniseries *Moon Knight* (2022), Oscar Isaac as Marc Specter (aka Moon Knight) drifts through multiple identities—Egyptian, Jewish, British-accented—but his Guatemalan Cuban heritage is narratively invisible. Zoe Saldaña's Gamora is literally painted green, her Latinidad erased in a wash of extraterrestrial abstraction. This practice, which media scholars Mary Beltrán and Camilla Fojas variously discuss as racial and ethnic ambiguity, allows studios to benefit from diversity optics without engaging the cultural specificity that genuine representation requires.

This phenomenon isn't limited to Marvel. The DC Universe similarly engages in a troubling sleight of hand—appropriating Latinx and Indigenous mythologies while sidestepping any meaningful acknowledgment or cultural engagement. Consider Batman, a figure routinely linked to the pulp legacy of Zorro yet rarely connected to one of Zorro's foundational inspirations: the corrido-like legend of Joaquín Murrieta.

Murrieta—Peter's great-great-great-great-grandfather—was a nineteenth-century Mexican bandit-hero whose mythos arose from the racial violence and dispossession inflicted by Anglo settler colonialism during and after the U.S. annexation of California. His life, defined by profound personal loss (his wife was raped and murdered by white settlers), systemic injustice, and resistance, became a narrative of survival and self-determined justice. Murrieta's story circulated widely in oral ballads and regional lore, eventually inspiring Johnston McCulley's creation of Zorro—a character that would become the template for masked vigilantes like Batman.

Yet in Batman's official mythos, this Latinx lineage is conspicuously absent. The figure of Murrieta—so central to the genealogy of the American superhero—is erased, replaced by narratives that elevate white trauma and morality while rendering brown resistance invisible. This erasure is not accidental. It reflects a broader tendency in mainstream media to mine Black, Indigenous, and People of Color (BIPOC) histories and aesthetics for symbolic depth while refusing to center or credit their cultural origins.

We see this hollowed-out mythology on full display in Christopher Nolan's *Batman Begins* (2005). As Frederick discusses in his *Latinx Superheroes in Mainstream Comics*, Nolan, to his credit, does make an attempt (albeit fleeting) to complicate the bat-suited white-savior narrative by inserting a subtle Indigenous subtext into Bruce Wayne's origin story. As a child, Bruce discovers a Native American arrowhead while playing on the Wayne estate—an artifact from a civilization long erased yet still haunting the soil beneath Gotham's elite. This moment, combined with Bruce's fall into the cave that later becomes the Batcave, creates an implicit narrative link between Wayne's transformation into Batman and the land's deeper, precolonial history.

Bruce gifts the arrowhead to his childhood friend Rachel Dawes—a gesture that acknowledges, however briefly, that the land he inherits and weaponizes was once inhabited and shaped by Indigenous peoples. Yet the film leaves this potential line of inquiry unexplored. There is no deeper engagement with the violent dispossession that made Wayne's privilege possible, nor with the symbolic weight of the arrowhead as a relic of colonial erasure. Instead, the object becomes a background prop—absorbed into the narrative of a white billionaire's trauma and self-actualization.

Nolan's gesture, while visually poetic, ultimately reproduces a troubling pattern: the invocation of Indigenous presence as aesthetic garnish rather than historical reckoning. The Batcave, symbol of Batman's transformation and power, is literally rooted in stolen land—but the mythology continues to center white legacy and moral exceptionalism. Rather than interrogate this origin, the film subsumes it under the logic of the white vigilante hero, reinforcing the idea that justice flows from personal trauma rather than structural history. As such, the arrowhead scene serves less as a critique and more as a quiet reinforcement of settler futurism, the notion that white narratives can inherit the symbols of the colonized without being accountable to the histories they signify.

This surface-level engagement with Indigenous history in *Batman Begins* is not an anomaly—it's part of a broader pattern in superhero media where non-Western cultures are mined for symbolic weight while remaining narratively marginal or outright invisible. If Christopher Nolan gestures toward this dynamic with a subtle nod—a Native American arrowhead in young Bruce Wayne's hand—Zack Snyder, by contrast, makes the white-optic appropriation unmistakably overt.

In *Justice League* (2017), Bruce Wayne strolls past encased samurai armor aboard his private jet, a visual tableau that echoes Edward Said's theory of Orientalism: how Western powers have historically constructed Asia as mystical, menacing, and other. These objects are not framed with reverence for their origins; instead, they operate as aesthetic trophies—tokens that elevate Bruce's cosmopolitan mystique. The armor, like so many borrowed visual cues across superhero franchises, functions less as cultural homage and more as narrative adornment. Snyder's vision reinforces the white-savior mythology—narratively, aesthetically, and politically—by showing us a hero whose dominance extends not just across villains, but across cultures

Lineages Erased, and Reclaimed

This cycle of cultural extraction operates without meaningful engagement, revealing how white-dominated industrial complexes continue to sideline Latinx and Indigenous histories. These industries view our rich cultural traditions as little more than symbolic repositories—convenient sources of narrative flair to be mined and repackaged. Mainstream film and TV persistently fail us in this regard, but Latinx comics offer something different: a visual and often powerfully alternative medium for storytelling. Comics become sites of resistance when filtered through ancestral memory rather than shaped by corporate imperatives.

Consider the mythic figure of the Camazotz, the bat god of death, night, and sacrifice from the K'iche' Maya *Popol Vuh*. In traditional accounts, Camazotz dwells in Zotzilaha (the House of Bats in Xibalba) and beheads one of the Maya Hero Twins, Hunahpú. This anthropomorphized bat deity represents primal force: simultaneously fearsome and sacred. Yet even before the K'iche' Maya recorded the Camazotz in the *Popol Vuh*, giant vampire bats were worshipped by the Zapotec people in Oaxaca as far back as AD 100, deeply embedding the deity in Mesoamerican cosmologies.

The Camazotz, then, is not simply a regional legend—it represents an erased origin story of the bat-hero archetype. While pulp magazines positioned Zorro as Batman's often-cited precursor, the Camazotz offers something much deeper and more ancient. Today's Latinx and Indigenous artists and writers are reclaiming this mythic force, fusing it with superhero tropes to produce dynamic, decolonial storytelling that has genuine stakes. Rafael Flores Jr. (writer) and Azrael Aguiar (illustrator) collaborate on the comic book series *The Return of Camazotz*. In this latter work, Flores blends metaphysics with the everyday, while Aguiar's expressionist visuals make each panel pulse with energy. The narrative reaches across time and space, finding spiritual continuities and contemporary relevance. In one striking sequence, a mother from Xibalba tells her son Víctor, "If you control it, Camazotz can be a force for good." Through moments like these, Flores recenters the Camazotz myth as a pathway to reimagine monstrosity, resist binary life-death cosmologies, and reclaim superheroes as a form of cultural stewardship. For Latinx audiences, these animated features and comics aren't merely entertainment—they become warrior-ancestors who haunt the underworld, drawing explicitly from these reclaimed cosmological roots.

We see this reclaiming taking shape in Mexico as well. Beginning with modernist Mexican printmaker Eliezer Canul and expanded by the likes of Yucatán artist and sculptor Christian Pacheco with his *Camazotz Batman* (a metal sculpture suit that embodies and fuses ancestral identity with contemporary pop aesthetics), we also see it in the work of artists like Erre Zetaka, who creates Maya-based mythological superhero digital art. These and others further expand these visual conversations, appealing to new generations of Mexicans who seek connections between ancestral knowledge and contemporary forms.

Even within mainstream-adjacent spaces, we see glimmers of this re-indigenization taking hold. Juan Meza-León's animated fea-

Figure 4 A joint production between Ánima Estudios and Warner Bros., *Batman Azteca* (2025) comes to Max to reclaim the beloved character's origins, rooted in the pre-Columbian legend of "Camazotz."

ture *Batman Azteca* (2025) imagines a new bat-hero: Yohualli Coatl (Horacio García Rojas), a priest-turned-vigilante operating in Moctezuma II's court. The film weaves the Batman myth through Nahua cosmology, with Hernán Cortés reimagined as a grotesque Two-Face-like conquistador and Yoka (Omar Chaparro) as a Jokeresque priest twisted by sacrificial ideology. While the remix may not reach the bat symbol's full radical potential, it nonetheless opens space for meaningful cultural reclamation within popular entertainment frameworks.

Futures That Almost Were

This brings us to another powerful figure who was almost centered: America Chavez, who first grew to prominence in Marvel Comics during the 2013 run of *Young Avengers*. Within the comics, she represents everything the MCU has consistently hesitated to embrace: brown, queer, defiant, and dazzlingly powerful. Originally created by Joe Casey and Nick Dragotta (*Vengeance* #1, 2011), America was later followed by Kieron Gillen's further development in his fifteen-issue run of *Young Avengers* (2013–2014), then fully realized by Gabby Rivera in *America* (2017–2018). Rivera added complexity to America's character and superpowers, layering additional dimensions of significance onto her identity as a being raised by two mothers, her ability to punch star-shaped portals between dimensions, and her existence as someone actively subverting heteronormative and nationalist norms. With Rivera's pen, America embodied what scholar José Esteban Muñoz once articulated as a queer futurity: a world "not yet here" but that we can nevertheless feel as we move toward it—the warm illumination of a horizon imbued with potentiality and promise. Rivera's America, followed by Kalinda Vazquez's 2021 run, gestured toward a language of Latinx lesbian superhero futures: vivid, tangible, and fully imagined.

Rivera's run deserves special attention here because it didn't just add Latinx representation to the Marvel universe. It fundamentally reimagined what superhero storytelling could be. The dialogue crackled with Spanglish authenticity. America called her mothers *mamis.* She moved through Washington Heights with the kind of spatial knowledge that only comes from actually living in a community, not just visiting it for a plot point. Rivera understood something crucial: You can't just drop a Latina character into a white narrative framework and call it representation. The entire storytelling grammar needs to shift. The pacing, the emotional beats, the humor, the way conflict resolves—all of it gets filtered through lived cultural experience.

And here's what made it revolutionary: America wasn't dealing with immigration trauma or gang violence or any of the usual "Latinx issues" that Hollywood loves to traffic in. She was dealing with cosmic-level threats, interdimensional ethics, and queer coming of age—all while being unapologetically Latinx. That's the future we're talking about. Not Latinx stories as sociological case studies, but Latinx characters at the center of any story, bringing our full complexity to bear on whatever genre we're working in.

When *Doctor Strange in the Multiverse of Madness* (2022) introduced America (Xochitl Gomez), Latinx fans held their collective breath. Would this onscreen version carry the radical charge of Rivera's comic run? The answer, heartbreakingly, was mixed. Xochitl Gomez's portrayal was sincere and spirited, but the script turned America into a plot device: her interdimensional powers were deployed to serve *Doctor Strange*'s arc rather than allowing her to exist as fully realized in her own right. Her queerness, while central to the comics, became largely invisible on screen. Her ethnic and cultural specificity was similarly diminished.

Peter remembers the exact moment in the theater when he realized what was happening. "There's this scene where Strange is basically mansplaining the multiverse to America—to America Chavez, who literally punches holes between dimensions. And I'm sitting there thinking, 'This is it. This is the writers' room dynamic playing out on screen.' The brown girl knows something the white guy doesn't, but we still have to center his journey, his learning, his redemption arc."

Frederick, who discusses America as a Latinx figure of futurity and empowerment, watched the film with Corina, his daughter, who'd grown up on Rivera's America Chavez. Her response was telling: "Why didn't they let her be the hero of her own story like in the comic books?" It's a question that continues to haunt MCU storytelling with growing urgency. Why are Latinx characters so often positioned as supporting players, always orbiting someone else's narrative center of gravity?

The answer, we've learned, isn't simply about individual creative decisions. It's structural. It's about who gets to be in the writers' room when the early story breaks happen. It's about which characters feel "relatable" to executives who've never had to code-switch. It's about marketing departments worried about the international box office, as if Latinx characters somehow don't play globally—a premise that's both racist and demonstrably false given the worldwide success of films like *Coco* and *Encanto*.

Peter, too, has witnessed this dynamic firsthand in writers' rooms. Latinx characters often begin with rich cultural specificity and genuine complexity, only to be "streamlined" in later drafts—a euphemism for erasure. What gets cut? Not the superpowers or the action sequences, but the anchor points: the ancestry, the cultural nuances, America's journey as both queer and Latina. From comic book hero to sidelined MCU sidekick, this trajectory illustrates the industry's persistent flattening of Latinx potential and cultural depth.

"I've literally been in rooms," Peter shares, "where someone pitches a beautiful, culturally specific moment—maybe the character's *abuela* gives them advice that reframes the whole mission, or they stop at a *panadería* and the interaction there reveals something crucial about who they are. And someone else in the room says, 'I love it, but does it move the plot forward?' As if character is plot. As if the cultural specificity isn't exactly what makes the story worth telling in the first place."

On the set of *Wizards,* there was once a poster in the living room that announced something aspirational: "Travel to Mexico," and the question came down repeatedly, "Are the Russos Mexican? Can't they be just *Latinx*?" We think if you can show us the country "Latinx" on a map, then sure. Otherwise, let us be us—fully, authentically, without apology.

This speaks to a deeper issue about how the industry understands—or misunderstands—cultural identity. There's this notion that being "too specific" somehow limits appeal, that universal stories require culturally neutral characters. But that's backward. The most universal stories are often the most culturally specific. *Coco* works precisely because it's deeply rooted in Mexican traditions around Día de los Muertos, not in spite of it. The specificity is the universality.

Before moving on, we want to spotlight Claire Temple, the African American doctor introduced in *Luke Cage, Hero for Hire* #2 (1972) and reimagined, with elements of the comic's Night Nurse, across the Marvel Defenders Netflix series (*Daredevil, Jessica Jones, Luke Cage, Iron Fist,* and *The Defenders*). Recast as a nurse and embodied by Afro-Latina actress Rosario Dawson, of Puerto Rican and Cuban descent, Claire became an Afro-Latinx revision of the character, breathing complexity into a role extending far beyond superhuman sidekick. She called out the heroes' self-destructiveness and recklessness, maintained her own moral center amid chaos, and navigated multiple communities with code-switching finesse that felt authentic to bicultural experience.

What Dawson brought to Claire Temple matters because it showed what's possible when a talented Latina actor gets material she can actually work with. Claire wasn't just "the girlfriend" or "the helper"—she had her own professional expertise, her own ethical framework, her own reasons for being in these stories. She moved between Hell's Kitchen's superhero world and her hospital's bureaucratic realities with a kind of bilingual fluency that many of us recognize from our own lives.

Yet despite her significance as a landmark Latina character in the MCU's early streaming ventures, she remained fundamentally a supporting figure—defined more by her relationships to the (predominantly male) heroes she aided than by her own narrative arc and aspirations. We never got Claire Temple's origin story. We never got to see her world, her family, her history as the primary focus. She was always in service to someone else's journey.

And here's the thing that frustrates us most: Claire Temple had decades of comic book history to draw from. The character has been around since the 1970s. There was source material. There were storylines. But even with all that foundation, even with Rosario Dawson's magnetic performance, the industry couldn't quite imagine centering her story. She could anchor scenes, provide emotional depth, offer crucial assistance—but she couldn't be the protagonist.

The pattern persists: Latinx characters who promise radical representation often become narrative satellites, their cultural specificity gradually dimmed to serve other storylines. We see it with America Chavez reduced to a plot device. We see it in Claire Temple, confined to supporting roles. We see it across the MCU and broader Hollywood landscape, where Latinx characters are allowed to exist but rarely allowed to truly lead.

We keep asking: When will the industry trust Latinx characters to carry their own stories forward, to exist at the center rather than the margins? When will "almost centered" finally become actually centered? And perhaps more importantly: What are we losing as audiences when these stories remain untold, when these characters remain underdeveloped, when these futures remain unrealized?

Because here's what we know from the comics: When Latinx creators get the chance to tell Latinx stories with Latinx characters at the center, magic happens. The storytelling becomes richer, more surprising, more emotionally resonant. Not because these stories are only "for" Latinx audiences, but because specificity and authenticity create the conditions for genuine connection across difference.

Superhero Darkside

If the MCU represents corporate liberalism's approach to diversity—inclusion as market expansion—Amazon's *The Boys* (2019–2026) and its spin-off *Gen V* (2023–) offer a cynical counternarrative. These shows deconstruct superhero mythology not just in terms of violence and ideology but also in how they handle race, gender, and sexuality. In this universe, corporate-manufactured diversity initiatives are performative gestures, designed to rebrand fascist power structures in palatable terms. Rainbow capitalism becomes a marketing scheme; Black and queer superheroes are commodified symbols used to conceal exploitation; and identity politics are absorbed into the very systems of surveillance, militarization, and celebrity spectacle that the shows critique.

Yet despite their sharp satire, both *The Boys* and *Gen V* fall into familiar traps of erasure and tokenism. While the shows gleefully dismantle the hypocrisies of corporate inclusion, they fail to imagine genuine alternatives. Latinx characters remain almost entirely absent from the narrative universe. In five seasons of *The Boys*, there is no Latinx character in a significant or sustained role. *Gen V* offers slightly more racial diversity among its younger cast, but Latinx presence is once again marginal at best—relegated to minor, unnamed, or stereotyped roles. The absence is especially glaring given the show's stated ambition to satirize U.S. institutions. It's easier, it seems, to envision a fascist superhero-industrial complex than to depict Latinx people as fully realized participants in these speculative worlds.

This absence reflects what Frances Negrón-Muntaner and her team of researchers at Columbia University term the "Latino media gap"—a structural failure of inclusion that goes beyond underrepresentation to encompass systematic erasure. In an entertainment landscape supposedly hungry for diverse voices, Latinx characters are not simply missing; they are excluded from the imaginary altogether. Even within a narrative that prides itself on challenging power, parodying neoliberalism, and exposing white supremacist logics, Latinx subjectivity remains unimaginable. The irony is profound: We exist in the real America that *The Boys* claims to satirize, yet we are nowhere to be found in its fictional mirror.

And here's what makes this particularly galling: The creative teams behind these shows aren't oblivious to representation politics. They're actively engaging with questions about race, gender, and sexuality. The shows feature extensive commentary on how corporations weaponize diversity. They understand performative allyship. They can identify and critique shallow inclusion. But somehow, in all that critical awareness, they never turned that lens on their own narrative choices. They never asked: "Who are we leaving out of this story about who gets left out?"

In this way, *The Boys* and *Gen V* reveal the limits of so-called radical media under capitalism. Representation is not just about optics or even access; it is about narrative possibility—and this narrative possibility, for us as Latinx scholars, teachers, creatives, and parents, means that Latinx characters are not only included but given narrative agency.

We want to see Latinx characters who aren't just reactive but proactive. Those who don't just respond to the corrupt systems but actively strategize against them, organize resistance, and imagine alternatives. We want to see the supes who are Mexican American, Puerto Rican, Dominican, or Salvadoran, bringing their specific cultural knowledge and community-organizing traditions to bear on superhero narratives. Because here's the thing: Latinx communities have long histories of resistance to corporate exploitation, militarization, and state violence. We have frameworks for understanding power that don't begin and end with white liberal critique.

What would *The Boys* look like if it included a Latinx character who understood Vought International's exploitation through the lens of United Farm Workers organizing, or sanctuary city movements, or Puerto Rican resistance to colonial capitalism? What if *Gen V* featured Latinx students whose critique of the university drew from generations of Chicana/o student activism, from the 1968 walkouts to contemporary immigrant rights organizing? These aren't just "diversity additions"—they're fundamentally different ways of understanding power, resistance, and transformation.

The absence of these perspectives doesn't just limit the shows' representational inclusivity; it limits their critical range. By imagining resistance only through frameworks already legible to white liberal audiences, these shows reproduce a kind of epistemological narrowness that undermines their own satirical ambitions. They can identify the problem but can't imagine solutions beyond the conceptual vocabulary that created the problem in the first place.

This is what we mean by narrative *agency* versus narrative *presence*. It's not enough to have Latinx characters appear on screen. They need to be architects of the story's moral and imaginative universe.

Beyond the Binary

The conversation about representation too often gets stuck in a binary: Is this good or bad representation? Does it uplift or stereotype? But as both of us have learned—Frederick through scholarship, Peter through creative practice—the more urgent and generative questions concern complexity, agency, and narrative power. Representation isn't just about showing up on the screen or the page; it's about how characters are built, what storylines they carry, what worlds they're allowed to inhabit and shape.

We already mentioned, in passing, Jeremy Slater's MCU miniseries *Moon Knight,* which provides Oscar Isaac with compelling material to explore intersectional identity issues, particularly ethnoracial and dissociative disorders. It's a layered, often nuanced portrayal that treats its protagonist with a certain dignity, even as it depicts his disintegration. But the show's reluctance to engage with Isaac's Guatemalan Cuban heritage—especially given how centrally the body and identity are at stake in the story—feels like a significant omission. Marc Spector's Jewish background is faintly referenced, yet the full intersection of his Jewish and Latin American identities, particularly within a narrative so embedded in Egyptian mythology, is never explored.

We've had long conversations about how there's something almost defensive in how the show handles Marc's ethnicity. Like they're afraid that acknowledging his Guatemalan heritage would somehow diminish the universality of his struggle with dissociative identity disorder. But that's exactly backward. The specificity of how identity fractures under trauma is always cultural. Jewish trauma has specific historical coordinates. Guatemalan displacement and the diaspora have their own genealogies. In fact, Peter pitched a show where the protagonist was dealing with intergenerational trauma, and the network loved it—until he made clear the character was Salvadoran and the trauma was connected to the civil war and U.S. intervention in El Salvador. Suddenly it was too political or "too specific." But a white character dealing with intergenerational Holocaust trauma or Irish immigration struggles? That's universal and deeply human.

And that silence is revealing. In *Latinx Superheroes in Mainstream Comics,* Frederick examines how even the most progressive or psychologically nuanced Latinx characters often remain trapped within an Anglocentric, monolithic cultural frame. Latinx superheroes, when they do appear, are frequently stripped of their cultural specificities, flattened into palatable figures designed for a generalized market. They are either overcoded with tropes—hypersexuality, machismo, exotic mysticism—or rendered faceless and placeless. When a show like *Moon Knight* avoids acknowledging its lead actor's ethnicity, it implicitly affirms that Latinx identity is either irrelevant to the narrative or too burdensome for audiences to handle.

But what if it weren't? What if Marc Spector's struggles with identity fragmentation were refracted through his bicultural heritage? What if the dislocations of trauma and the multiplicity of the self were informed not only by his mental health but also by the liminal space of being Latinx and Jewish in a world that resists hybrid identities? As Frederick argues elsewhere, Latinx superheroes often exist in liminal zones where bicultural, bilingual, and border-crossing experiences challenge the rigid binaries of good-evil, self-other, and normal-abnormal. This narrative space is rich with metaphorical potential—especially for stories like *Moon Knight*, which already wrestle with fractured selves and mythic burdens.

The show gestures toward this complexity through its Egyptian mythology framework, which already asks viewers to accept multiple realities and identities coexisting simultaneously. Marc is also Steven. Steven is also Jake. They share a body but experience reality differently. That's already a narrative that demands comfort with multiplicity. So why not extend that same generosity to cultural multiplicity? Why not let Marc's Guatemalan heritage and Jewish identity be in genuine conversation with each other, inflecting his experience of trauma, memory, and healing?

These aren't just academic questions. Peter has repeatedly pitched stories that foreground such hybrid identities—characters whose powers dramatize the tensions and fluidities of bicultural life—only to be told they're too niche, too complex, or not relatable enough. But this pushback reveals a profound misunderstanding of how storytelling works. Specificity is not a barrier to connection; it is its engine. When audiences see a character deeply rooted in cultural specificity, it opens new emotional and narrative pathways.

And yet we can't help but think about the many people like us who connected with *Moon Knight* who didn't have dissociative identity disorder. They connected because the show dramatized internal fragmentation in ways that felt emotionally true even if not literally autobiographical. The same would be true for cultural specificity. You don't need to be Guatemalan or Jewish to understand what it means to carry histories that don't fit neatly into the dominant culture's categories. You don't need to be bicultural to understand the code-switching, the translation, and the constant negotiation between different versions of self. These are deeply human experiences; they just happen to take culturally specific forms.

As Frederick's research shows, the most enduring and beloved Latinx superhero characters—like Miles Morales, America Chavez in the comics, and Jaime Reyes's Blue Beetle—aren't just those who appear onscreen but those whose narrative arcs are inseparable from their cultural identities. Their powers, their conflicts, and their moral frameworks are shaped by being Latinx so inextricably that removing it would change who they are.

Miles Morales works because his Brooklyn is a specific Brooklyn: Afro-Latino, bilingual, working-class. His relationships with his parents, his uncle, and his community all inform how he understands responsibility, legacy, and heroism. When the animated *Spider-Man: Into the Spider-Verse* (2018) leaned into that specificity rather than away from it, the film became a global phenomenon. Not despite its cultural particularity, but because of it.

Similarly, Jaime Reyes as Blue Beetle succeeds in the comics when writers understand that his working-class Mexican American family dynamics aren't set dressing: they're central to how he processes power, responsibility, and transformation. The alien scarab chooses him, but how he wields that power is shaped by his family's values, their economic struggles, and their immigration history. That's not "too specific"—that's what makes the character resonate.

The 2023 film *Blue Beetle,* despite its production and distribution challenges, demonstrated this principle. When Jaime's family becomes integral to the narrative—not just supportive but actively involved in the superhero journey—the story gains emotional weight and cultural authenticity. His *abuela* isn't just comic relief; she's a carrier of intergenerational wisdom and resistance. His parents' economic anxiety isn't just background; it's the context that makes Jaime's choices meaningful.

What *Moon Knight* missed was this opportunity. Oscar Isaac brought depth and commitment to the role, but the writing never fully trusted that his Guatemalan Jewish identity could be *the* thing rather than *a* thing. The show wanted to be universal, but in its reach for universality, it actually narrowed its emotional and imaginative range.

One Step Forward, Two Back

And here's what frustrates us: The tools for telling these stories already exist. Latinx comics creators have been developing these narrative strategies for decades. As comic book writers, we join those like Gabby Rivera and others mentioned in weaving cultural specificity into superhero narratives in ways that deepen rather than limit their appeal. Working with and alongside extraordinary Latinx artists like Miguel Hernández, Lalo Alcaraz, Jaime Hernandez, and others, we've seen firsthand how our words transform into visualized Latinx storyworlds with both specificity and expansiveness.

The issue isn't that mainstream productions don't know how to tell these stories; it's that they don't trust audiences to receive them. There's this persistent belief that specificity alienates, that cultural particularity is niche, that "universal" means culturally neutral (which really means white and Anglo). But every successful piece of culturally specific storytelling proves this assumption wrong.

As we write this, the streaming landscape is more saturated than ever, with platforms like Disney+ doubling down on Marvel's recent Phase Five *Agatha All Along* (2024), *Ironheart* (2025), and *Daredevil: Born Again* (2025), among others. On the surface, these titles suggest a meaningful move toward diversity. Yet beneath the promotional gloss, a deeper pattern persists: Latinx characters remain largely sidelined from positions of narrative centrality and complexity.

Consider the *Eternals* (2021), where Salma Hayek's Ajak, cast as a wise spiritual guide, holds symbolic importance but receives minimal screen time before being unceremoniously killed off. Her death, while meant to raise the stakes, also eliminates a rare example of a visibly older Latina superhero with agency. We already mentioned in passing how dimension-hopping, time-traveling America Chavez appears in Sam Raimi's *Doctor Strange in the Multiverse of Madness* (2022); she barely gets screen time and lacks agency and a textured backstory. Her inclusion feels more like a plot device than a character we're meant to invest in. Once again: Latinx superheroes in lost functionary limbo.

In the Marvel Phase Four *Werewolf by Night* (2022), Gael García Bernal steps into a rare spotlight role as Jack Russell. The Halloween special offers a stylistic break from MCU norms, drenched in black and white and full of gothic flourishes. But its placement as a one-off, largely disconnected from Marvel's broader narrative web, makes it feel more like an aesthetic experiment than a platform for lasting representation. Once again, a Latinx superhero is quarantined in the margins.

Meanwhile, *Echo* (2024) marked an unprecedented moment in the MCU: a series fronted by Alaqua Cox as Maya Lopez, a deaf Indigenous woman introduced in *Hawkeye* (2021). The series earned praise for foregrounding Indigenous culture and using American Sign Language with authenticity. It is worth noting how few Latinx characters framed the story, even on screen. Although Maya Lopez is much more centered and even tied to Latinx heritage in the comics (depending on the creative run), this dimension is almost erased. Instead, *Echo* gains far more by embracing her Indigenous background over Indigenous inclusion, leaving the broader Latinx superhero lineage again in limbo.

There was, however, a glimmer of potential in *Daredevil: Born Again*, where we witnessed the proverbial baton being passed from Hector Ayala as White Tiger (played by the late Puerto Rican actor Kamar de los Reyes) to the niece, Angela del Toro (played by Puerto Rican actor Camila Rodriguez). Although this succession marks one of the rare times the MCU has acknowledged the intergenerational, legacy-driven nature of Latinx superheroes in the comics, Reyes's appearance is limited to a few episodes, offering fans a glimpse of what a sustained, culturally grounded Latinx hero narrative could look like in the MCU. But anytime the narrative moved into real explorations of tributes, inheritances, and communitary protection, central tenets of Latinx comic storytelling, her presence evaporated by season's end, even after Ayala's death.

Yet even this promising arc reinforces the broader frustration: that Latinx superheroes often exist only in the shadow of loss. Their presence is spectral, appearing briefly, then vanishing, leaving behind echoes more than legacies. Reyes's White Tiger, like Ajak in *Eternals*, exists for a moment and then disappears. The pattern speaks volumes: Latinx heroes are allowed to exist, but not to endure. They can appear, but they cannot anchor. They can contribute, but they cannot lead.

Coco didn't succeed by being "universal" in some abstract sense—it succeeded by being deeply, specifically Mexican in its engagement with Día de los Muertos, family structure, music, and memory. *Encanto* didn't become a phenomenon by diluting Colombian culture—it leaned in, trusting audiences to connect with the specificity. These films prove that when you trust the audience with cultural complexity, when you don't condescend or overexplain, something magical happens. The specificity becomes the bridge, not the barrier.

So when *Moon Knight* sidesteps Marc Spector's Guatemalan heritage, or when *Eternals* kills off Ajak before we truly know her, or when *Echo* erases Maya Lopez's Latinx comic book heritage, or when White Tiger appears for just a handful of episodes—these aren't just missed opportunities for representation. They're missed opportunities for richer storytelling. The MCU wants to explore complex identities but doesn't fully commit to exploring how identity shapes narrative agency differently across different cultural contexts.

We agree that a critique of good versus bad representation misses the point. The question is always: Does this character's identity inform their narrative agency? Do they get to shape the storyworld, or does the storyworld just happen around them? Are they architects or ornaments? The MCU keeps giving us protagonists with enormous potential for cultural complexity, yet treats that complexity as irrelevant to their actual journeys. That's not neutral; that's a choice with consequences.

And those consequences matter because they accumulate. Each time a show chooses to sideline cultural specificity, each time a character's ethnicity is treated as incidental rather than fundamental, each time complexity is sacrificed for supposed universality, we lose a little more imaginative possibility. We lose the chance to show audiences—Latinx and otherwise—that our stories, in all their cultural particularity, are worthy of being centered, worthy of shaping narrative worlds, worthy of being more than afterthoughts or spectral presences in someone else's journey.

The pattern reveals itself across Phase Four and Phase Five: one step forward in acknowledging Latinx existence, two steps back in denying us narrative centrality and sustained presence. The MCU can imagine us, briefly. It can gesture toward our stories, fleetingly.

Heroes Born

The relationship between comics and the MCU reveals both promising pathways and persistent roadblocks for Latinx representation. In the comics medium, creators often have more space to experiment: to take narrative risks, develop character depth, and build audiences gradually. Miles Morales spent years finding his voice on the page before becoming a multimedia phenomenon. America Chavez was allowed multiple series (though unevenly received) that deepened her mythology. Jaime Reyes's evolution from a supporting legacy character to a solo hero with his own title exemplifies the slow-build development pipeline available in comics.

This development pipeline can serve as a proving ground for broader media visibility. In comics, where monthly sales of 30,000 copies can sustain a title, Latinx characters can be cultivated with narrative specificity and cultural grounding. But once they're transitioned to film, they enter a realm of blockbuster expectations, where anything short of $300 million is framed as failure. This scale shift invites—and often demands—a flattening of cultural specificity. "Universal appeal" becomes code for generic storytelling. Gatekeepers question the "relatability" of a bicultural narrative or the commercial viability of code-switching English-Spanish dialogue. Latinidad, if acknowledged at all, is often made ornamental or exotic.

We weren't the only ones excited at the news of a *Blue Beetle* feature film (released in 2023). It ignited excitement within Latinx communities across the country. It also triggered the usual apprehension. Would Jaime Reyes's El Paso roots, a key part of his character's cultural geography, survive the transition to the screen? Would his family remain central to his arc, or be reduced to background texture? Peter, who had friends working on the project, heard familiar internal studio conversations: How much Spanish was too much? Would audiences need subtitles to understand the scarab speaking in Spanish? Could they show Mexican life without sepia filters and poverty porn?

Once it dropped in 2023, Ángel Manuel Soto's *Blue Beetle* offered a case study of both the gains and the gaps in Latinx representation.

On the one hand, the film made a bold move with its color-conscious casting, proudly placing brown-skinned, multilingual, working-class characters at the heart of a DC superhero origin story. Adriana Barraza's *abuela* (Nana) and George Lopez's *tío* Rudy are not punchlines or sidekicks; they're sources of strength, history, and sometimes outright rebellion. The film even weaves in a brilliant nod to *El Chapulín Colorado*, the beloved Mexican superhero parody, in the design of Jaime's costume—an act of visual homage that places Mexican cultural production at the heart of the superhero genre. The revelation of Nana's past as a soldadera (female revolutionary fighter) during the Mexican Revolution is another rare moment of historical depth in a genre that too often ignores Latin American histories altogether. And the soundtrack: Wow! It features Puerto Rican hip-hop group Calle 13, norteño legends Los Tucanes de Tijuana, and cumbia-ska-reggae fusion from Celso Piña, creating a Latinx audioscape that powerfully underscores the vibrant, Latinx transhemispheric sonic identity rarely experienced in big-budget superhero films.

But for all these triumphs, the film also made concessions that disappointed. Rather than setting the story in El Paso—a city loaded with symbolic and geopolitical resonance for U.S.-Mexico border culture—the film introduces a fictional tropical metropolis, Palmera City, a pan-Latino blend that reads more like Miami than a border town. El Paso survives only as a street sign, and the specific textures of border life are replaced with generic sci-fi skylines.

As we've endlessly discussed, this kind of relocation is not neutral. It displaces Latinx narratives from contested real spaces into sanitized fantasy worlds, muting the cultural and political tensions that give stories like *Blue Beetle* their charge. In other words, it relocates Latinx struggle from the borderlands to a safe, exotic imaginary.

Still, there are powerful moments of resistance. Ignacio Carapax's arc—shifting from corporate soldier to a figure of decolonial rebellion against Victoria Kord, the embodiment of white capitalist exploitation—offers a potent metaphor for liberation. Kord's weaponization of alien technology and desire to control the scarab mirror real-world patterns of imperial extraction. Carapax's final act is one of refusal: to kill, to obey, to perpetuate systems of domination. That a character marked as the film's antagonist is given a redemptive, anticolonial trajectory speaks to the film's more radical undercurrents.

Figure 5 *Blue Beetle* (2023) allows not only Jaime Reyes (Xolo Maridueña) to shine but also emphasizes his very important dynamic with family members (Adriana Barraza, Damián Alcázar, Elpidia Carrillo, Belissa Escobedo, and George Lopez).

Ultimately, *Blue Beetle* represents both progress and compromise. It succeeds in casting Latinx identity as central, rather than peripheral, to a superhero's emotional and familial life. But it also reveals how cultural specificity is still seen as a risk in Hollywood, requiring mitigation through generic tropes and invented cities. *Blue Beetle* reminds us that representation alone isn't enough. What matters isn't who appears on the page or screen but who shapes the storyworld and whose histories are allowed to matter. *Blue Beetle* gives us a glimpse of what's possible when Latinx creators and performers are allowed to lead, and points to the ongoing need to demand not only visibility, but narrative agency.

The DEI Paradox

Peter's experience pitching and developing projects for streamers underscores this frustrating paradox. While DEI mandates are important—nothing would change without these kinds of forceful initiatives—they can create the appearance of progress but come laden with qualifiers: The project must be "four-quadrant" (appealing to all demographics), have "global appeal" (which usually means stripping out local specificity), and meet "key metrics" (which often hinge on white audience engagement). As one development executive candidly described it, the result is often "diversity-flavored vanilla"—a product that appears inclusive on the surface but offers familiar, risk-averse narratives beneath the surface.

The HBO Max series *Gordita Chronicles* (2022), created by Claudia Forestieri and produced by Eva Longoria, is a painful example of this contradiction. A warm and well-written coming-of-age sitcom centered on a Dominican American girl in 1980s Miami, *Gordita Chronicles* was canceled after one season despite positive reviews and a dedicated fan base. The reason? It didn't fit the platform's rebranded "global strategy." That Latinx-centered stories are deemed incompatible with "global" shows how market logic continues to erase marginalized voices, even as it claims to amplify them.

Similarly, Netflix's *Gentefied* (2020–2021) and *On My Block* (2018–2021) drew critical praise for telling nuanced, intergenerational Latinx stories set in Boyle Heights and South-Central L.A., respectively. Both shows balanced humor with sharp commentary on gentrification, identity, and systemic inequality. Yet both were ultimately canceled, signaling how even "successful" shows—according to qualitative measures—are vulnerable to short-term data analytics that fail to account for long-tail cultural value.

The way we see it, the broader problem is this: Latinx representation has been siloed into "niche" storytelling rather than integrated into the central mythologies of American pop culture. As Frederick discusses in his various books on Latinx comics, film, and TV, the move toward inclusion without structural change replicates hegemonic systems of symbolic and economic control. It allows the industry to appear progressive while maintaining existing hierarchies of cultural production. A character like America Chavez may exist in the multiverse, but her narrative agency is still constrained by white-authored scripts and strategic ambiguity. These stories give us representation without reckoning, inclusion without redistribution.

Our Superheroes

Perhaps the most revolutionary aspect of the MCU era isn't what Marvel has done, but how Latinx communities have responded, reshaped, and reimagined superhero culture on their own terms. While the MCU doles out representation in cautious increments, Latinx fans, creators, and scholars have been building a parallel cultural infrastructure rooted in joy, resistance, and creative agency.

Fanfic platforms like Archive of Our Own (AO3) are rich with speculative stories that reimagine characters like America Chavez with deeper cultural and queer specificity than the studio version dared to explore. TikTok creators and YouTubers now command audiences that rival viewership for some Disney+ releases, leveraging humor, critique, and cosplay to celebrate Latinx nerd culture and expose media blind spots. In these grassroots spaces, community replaces corporate branding, and creativity flourishes beyond the limits of studio-approved narratives.

Homegrown conventions—such as the Latino Comics Expo, The Latinx Comics Arts Festival, Texas Latino Comic Con, and Frederick's own BIPOC PoP: Comics, Gaming, Animation, and Multimedia Arts Expo & Symposium—have become vital ecosystems of cultural production. These are not merely alternative fan spaces; they are knowledge-sharing hubs, incubators of artistic careers, and laboratories of representation. They host panel discussions on Afro-Latinidad in comics, zine-making workshops for emerging creators, and conversations about queering superhero archetypes. They're also where brown kids and teens don costumes that reflect who they are and who they want to become.

At BIPOC PoP, we regularly see Latinx cosplayers celebrate both original Latinx superheroes—like Jessica Cruz as Green Lantern, Jaime Reyes as Blue Beetle, and Angela and Ava Ayala as White Tiger—as well as reinhabit classic superheroes like Batman with Michael Garcia as Chicano Batman, Wonder Woman, and Spider-Man in ways that decenter whiteness and open up mythic space. These cosplay acts are more than dress-up; they are acts of reclamation. As frequent BIPOC PoP cosplayer and Dallas denizen Amazon Daniella (@amazon.daniella) has remarked: "We, too, belong in these universes."

These conventions have created new knowledge economies. Latinx scholars, artists, and writers gather not only to celebrate but also to publish, organize, and mentor. Strategies for breaking into the comics industry are exchanged alongside self-published graphic novels. You see creators of all ages at artist alley tables, selling their work directly to readers, circumventing the corporate bottlenecks that have long excluded marginalized voices. And you see something else too: the spark in a kid's eyes when they recognize themselves in the *Blue Beetle* comics and merch, surrounded by a community that affirms that belonging.

This isn't just happening in the spaces we're creating, curating, and participating in. In the classroom and in our creative and scholarly work, we both teach and practice counterstorytelling to foreground the voices and experiences left out of dominant narratives. We're not sitting around waiting for change. In our multipronged push, together with our communities, we're creating spaces where counterstorytelling becomes sites of Latinx creation and knowledge production. We're centering Latinx joy, cultural specificity, and authorial control. With every person we see creating their own Latinx superhero, every Latinx cosplayer, every Latinx fanfic creator giving America Chavez the narrative she deserves, every self-publishing Latinx comic creator, instead of waiting for the "big two" (Marvel and DC) to call, they are building a future where Latinx identities are not an exception, but foundational.

Shields We Carry

Sam Wilson as Captain America matters. Representation at that level shifts possibilities. But Isaiah Bradley's bitter wisdom matters too: Symbols without structural change are just prettier cages. The shield Sam carries is heavy with history, and the MCU's handling of Latinx representation carries its own weight of absence and potential.

As we look toward the MCU's next phases (we're currently in Phase Six), the question isn't whether we'll see more brown faces in superhero suits—we will, because the market demands it. The question is whether those heroes will carry our full humanity or just our surface features. Will America Chavez get to be the queer Latinx revolutionary the comics promised her to be, or will she remain a supporting player in someone else's multiverse? Will the next generation of heroes reflect the complexity of Latinx life, or will they be filtered through the same white-optic-shaping lens?

The answer lies partly in those corporate boardrooms and writers' rooms that Peter frequents as the lone Latinx creative. It also lies, however, in our communities' continued insistence on something better. Every time we celebrate authentic representation and call out its absence, we help reshape the cultural conversation. Every time we buy a comic created by Latinx artists and writers, we push the boundaries of what's possible. In doing so, we open doors for future generations—kids who not only wield protective shields but also come to see themselves as containing infinite superheroic potential.

Chapter 2

IDEAL VERSUS REAL AUDIENCES

Imagine this scenario. Peter sits in a pristine conference room in Burbank in 2019. Across from him, three executives—all white, all wearing variations of the same expensive casual clothes—lean forward with practiced interest. He's pitching a show about a Latinx dad and son running a food truck business, inspired by his own experiences as a *papá* with his sons. It's specific, it's heartfelt, it's based on real entrepreneurial triumph in the face of systemic barriers.

"We love it," says the lead executive, and Peter knows what's coming. "But could we make it more . . . universal?"

Universal. Peter hears this in every pitch meeting. Loosely translated, it means: *Make it white*. Or rather, make it palatable to the white audiences we imagine are the only real audiences. Never mind that Latinx households overindex in media consumption. Never mind that *Jane the Virgin* (2014–2019) and *One Day at a Time* (2017–2020) proved that culturally specific stories can reach broad, multiracial, multigenerational audiences. Never mind that a *primo*'s food truck serves lines of customers from every background—none of whom need the food "translated" to enjoy it.

"What if," the executive continues, "the teenage daughter is embarrassed by the family business? Wants to fit in at her prep school. That's universal—every teenager rebels against their parents!"

And there it is: the transformation of a story about Latinx entrepreneurial success into yet another aspirational assimilationist narrative. The real audience—Latinx families who see their own struggles and triumphs reflected—is erased in favor of the *ideal audience*: white viewers who need brown characters to perform palatability, not authenticity.

The entertainment industry continues to operate on a founding myth: the universal viewer. This mythical figure—still the default in most executive imaginations—is implicitly white, middle-class,

English-monolingual, and suburban. Stories must be relatable to this viewer, who is presumed to lack the curiosity or capacity to engage with experiences beyond their own. A few lines of unsubtitled Spanish might turn them off. A culturally specific setting might push them away. Authenticity, unless explained or softened, is considered a risk.

We encounter this myth not just in studios and pitch rooms, but also in academia. In Peter's screenwriting and representation courses at Arizona State University, and in Frederick's Latinx pop culture seminars at the University of Texas at Austin, one question inevitably surfaces, sometimes from colleagues, sometimes from administrators: *Is this material accessible to non-Latinx students*? The question reveals an underlying assumption: White students are the default audience for education, just as white viewers are presumed to be the default audience for entertainment. Meanwhile, Latinx students have spent their entire academic lives making themselves "accessible" to white-centered curricula, often without complaint, and rarely with reciprocal consideration.

But who, really, is this so-called universal viewer? It's not white viewers. According to the 2023 Nielsen's Diverse Intelligence Series report:

- Latinx viewers overindex on streaming, with 61 percent naming it their primary destination for TV viewing, higher than the general population.
- Latinx audiences spend nearly half their total TV time (48.9 percent) with streaming content, reflecting outsized appetite for on-demand video.
- Despite this engagement, Latinx viewers held just an 8.5 percent share of screen in streaming content, far below their share of the U.S. population.
- Latinx audiences were the most likely group to say media representation has declined in accuracy since 2021, even as their viewing share grows.

Despite these facts, Latinx representation in the media industry remains profoundly limited both on screen and behind the scenes. According to the USC Annenberg Inclusion Initiative's 2023 report, of the 1,600 top-grossing films released between 2007 and 2022, only

5.5 percent of speaking roles were filled by Hispanic/Latino characters, despite Latinx individuals making up nearly 19.1 percent of the U.S. population. The disparity is even greater when it comes to lead or co-lead roles, where Latinx actors were featured in just 4.4 percent of films. Behind the camera, the underrepresentation deepens: only 4.6 percent of all directors and a mere 3.1 percent of credited producers during this period were Latinx. These figures expose a systemic exclusion that persists despite the growing demographic and cultural presence of Latinx communities across the country.

These numbers are not only dismal, but they are also damning. They confirm what we've long known: The so-called universal viewer is an ideological fiction. A myth that props up a white-dominated creative infrastructure. If this imagined viewer must be white, then—by unspoken industry logic—those best equipped to write, direct, and greenlight stories must also be white.

Today's white-optic-shaped narratives ignore the facts by erasing the very audiences that sustain them. This goes beyond oversight, it's lazy storytelling. These narratives flatten the richness and complexity of storytelling possibilities, reducing our vibrant communities to stereotypes or invisibility. As Frederick observes in his Introduction to *Latinx TV in the Twenty-First Century*, the televisual-industrial complex manufactures "white, suburban, capitalistic, heteronormative family life as the norm" while simultaneously invisibilizing and hypervisibilizing Latinxs in ways that fracture how we perceive ourselves.

Burden of Being *Everything to Everyone All at Once*

Creating Latinx content in the white-optic-shaping media-industrial complex often comes with a set of contradictory and impossible expectations. Every project is expected to:

- Represent the entire Latinx diaspora (an impossibility given our vast racial, regional, linguistic, and generational diversity)
- Educate white audiences but not in a way that feels "preachy" or "political"
- Avoid stereotypes while still being "authentically Latinx"
- Achieve commercial success at the scale of global blockbusters to "prove" viability

- Be progressive but not "too political" or "alienating"
- Center Latinx stories but still be "universal" enough to appeal to everyone

This reflects what Mary Beltrán describes as the industry's "universal" storytelling imperative: that appeal-to-everyone trap in which a pan-ethnic framework dilutes Latinx stories, creates bland characters, and strips them of cultural specificity.

Frederick feels this burden constantly when pitching comics, children's books, and young adult novels. Mainstream publishers and non-Latinx editors often express enthusiasm for Latinx protagonists and culturally rooted storyworlds—until the stories begin to speak unapologetically from a Latinx perspective. When he submitted his bilingual children's book *Con Papá / With Papá*, his Spanish version of *The Adventures of Chupacabra Charlie*, and his young adult novel, *The Absolutely (Almost) True Adventures of Max Rodriguez*, to mainstream agents, he encountered a wall of hesitancy. The books featured code-switching, cultural specificity, and unexplained customs—precisely the richness that Latinx readers might recognize and celebrate. But to the agents, these elements triggered a flurry of red flags: "Will readers understand this?" "Should we add a glossary?" "Can you make it more palatable?" Unwilling to compromise on language, context, and audience, Frederick ultimately took these books to mid-sized independent and academic presses with fiction imprints—spaces more willing to trust the reader's intelligence and the integrity of the narrative.

Peter faces the same pressures in every writers' room. During his time working on Netflix's *Mr. Iglesias* (2019–2020), network executives' notes routinely asked for "clarity," which doubled as cultural erasure. Why wear a *quinceañera* dress to class? (Cultural practice must be explained.) Why do the students switch between English and Spanish? (Bilingualism must be justified.) Why does the family gather for Sunday dinner? (Cultural rituals must have a plot function.) These are questions no one asks of white, middle-class characters whose behaviors are treated as the neutral default. In these rooms, Latinx culture is treated not as story, but as "content," requiring annotation and justification. It's what Beltrán talks about as the heavy burden of representation, one white creators rarely face.

This double standard reveals the enduring racial hierarchy of narrative legibility. White characters are granted interiority, tradition, and eccentricity without having to explain themselves. Latinx characters must constantly translate their existence to be considered coherent. These demands amount to a form of narrative contortion—a bending of the Latinx self to fit into frameworks that were never built to hold us.

What's lost in this process isn't only authenticity, it's possibility. How do you write freely when your audience is presumed to be unfamiliar, skeptical, or hostile? How do you build a storyworld when you're forced to justify its every brick?

The answer, increasingly, lies in carving out creative spaces that don't require permission: academic presses, independent publishing, Latinx-owned media houses, or self-distribution. These spaces offer not just freedom from gatekeeping but the possibility of reimagining who the audience is and what storytelling can be.

We shouldn't have to choose between authenticity and access, between being culturally rich and commercially viable. We deserve to tell our stories in our own voices—without footnotes, apologies, or compromise.

Netflix's Revolution That Wasn't

When *One Day at a Time* was canceled by Netflix in March of 2019, it felt like a gut punch to Latinx audiences and creators alike. The show had accomplished something rare in contemporary TV: it centered a Cuban American family unapologetically. Under the stewardship of co-showrunners Gloria Calderón Kellett and Mike Royce, with Norman Lear as executive producer, the reboot took the traditional sitcom format and infused it with intergenerational complexity and political urgency. It explored immigration, post-traumatic stress disorder, queer identity, addiction, and mental health—not as issues of the week, but as lived experiences grounded in culture and community. As Beltrán discusses in *Latino TV: A History*, Calderón Kellett pushed for cultural specificity over the generic, pan-Latinx approach, fighting to make Netflix executives understand that the Alvarez family needed cultural depth, and she built narratives that wove intersectional identities (immigrant, queer, generational) into the texture of an ordinary American family. Rapid-fire Spanish flew without subtitles. References to Cuban history, Catholic guilt, and cultural food rituals landed without explanation. It trusted the audience to keep up—and we did.

What followed wasn't a revolution, but a familiar betrayal.

Despite glowing reviews and a passionate fan base, Netflix pulled the plug after three seasons. The show had done everything right: It earned critical acclaim, built an intergenerational audience, and modeled the kind of inclusive storytelling that diversity, equity, and inclusion pledges claim to champion. But it failed in the eyes of the algorithm. Netflix, trained on the behavioral data of its imagined "ideal" viewer—young, white, individual, binge-oriented—couldn't make sense of the way Latinx audiences showed up. We watched together, often in family gatherings or living rooms with shared logins—patterns that don't register cleanly as separate streams. We discussed episodes on Facebook, Instagram, and WhatsApp, not necessarily on Twitter or Reddit. Our engagement was deep but nonconforming. And in an industry increasingly governed by data over context, different meant invisible.

Its temporary rescue by Pop TV in 2020 felt like a miracle—and a warning. It revealed a hard truth about who counts in media ecosystems increasingly shaped by platform logic. The real audience for *One Day at a Time* was multigenerational, bilingual, and emotionally invested. This audience mobilized petitions, mounted fan campaigns, and organized communal watch parties. The ideal audience, as defined

Figure 6 Despite acclaim from both critics and fans, Netflix canceled *One Day at a Time* (2017–2020) after only three seasons.

by the algorithm, had already been served—and found wanting. Netflix's model favored bingeable, short-term engagement over sustained communal connection. What it couldn't quantify, it couldn't value.

The cancellation of *One Day at a Time* was not just the end of a show; it was a cautionary tale about the limits of algorithmic visibility. As Frederick has written elsewhere, platforms mistake data for meaning and end up privileging homogenized consumption over culturally specific storytelling. They thereby risk erasing the very communities they claim to uplift.

The show's legacy, however, endures. It carved out space for new kinds of representation, laid groundwork for future Latinx-led series, and proved that "niche" storytelling can carry universal emotional weight. It also galvanized audiences and creators to rethink where and how they invest their creative energy. Maybe the revolution didn't happen on Netflix—but it did happen in our classrooms, our community screenings, and our collective refusal to be rendered invisible by a flawed algorithm.

Gentefied (2020–2021) offered another test case in audience expectations. Created by Marvin Lemus and Linda Yvette Chávez for Netflix and premiering in February of 2020, the show tackled gentrification in Boyle Heights with nuance. It refused simple narratives of everyday Latinx life, even airing our dirty laundry, including the colorism and queerphobia that run in our communities. The characters were complex: Chicana/os who were both victims and agents of gentrification, who navigated art-world pretensions and community obligations, who code-switched not just linguistically but culturally.

Gentefied is canon in Frederick's Latinx pop culture courses, where Latinx students see their own negotiations reflected: the queer cousin who went to art school and now feels disconnected, the family business threatened by rising rents, the compromise between cultural preservation and economic survival, the struggles of mixed-status families. White students, initially confused by the lack of clear heroes and villains, gradually came to appreciate the complexity—but only through guided discussion.

This is the challenge: *Gentefied* assumed its audience could handle complexity, sit with discomfort, and recognize that gentrification isn't a problem with easy solutions. But Netflix, despite greenlighting the show, didn't trust audiences enough to give it more than two seasons, shutting it down in January of 2022. The algorithm demanded immediate, massive viewership, the kind that comes from broad appeal rather than deep connection.

Youth Storyworlds

The battle over audiences starts young. Peter's work as a writer, producer, and showrunner on *Wizards of Waverly Place* (2007–2012) revealed how desperately Latinx kids hunger for representation and how nervously executives approach providing it. The Russo family was written half Mexican, half Italian American, but network caution kept the Latinidad mostly to episodic gestures like the season 1 "Quinceañera," which we'll explore in chapter 6, with Peter's insider eye, as "representation by accident."

Yet young Latinx viewers claimed Alex anyway. They recognized something in Gomez's performance, in Alex's position as the overlooked middle child who was actually the most powerful, in her refusal to be the "good girl." Fanfic exploded with stories that made explicit what the show wouldn't: Alex as a proud Chicana witch, navigating both magical and cultural borders.

Frederick's daughter, now at the University of Texas at Austin, still talks about what Alex Russo meant to her at eight years old: "She looked like me and she was powerful and funny and got in trouble but was still loved." That's the real audience response—deep, personal, lasting. But Disney Channel, focused on their ideal audience (white suburban kids), never fully realized what they had.

On TikTok, creators like Cuban American comedians Jenny Lorenzo (@jenny_lorenzo) and Kat Stickler (@katstickler) create unapologetically specific content: bilingual, bicultural, and boldly, joyfully rooted in everyday Latinx experience. These creators rack up millions of views without translating, explaining, or softening their cultural frames. They perform for their real audience—other Latinx youth—and in doing so, find massive success.

The comment sections tell the story. Under a video about struggling with Spanish in academic settings, thousands respond with stories of linguistic shame and pride. Under a skit about navigating awkward questions from white friends about *quinceañeras* or tamales, viewers tag their *primos* with "this is literally us." The community creates itself, proves itself, sustains itself—all without studio approval, algorithmic favoritism, or industry greenlights.

In the Latinx Pop Lab on campus, Frederick watches his daughter Corina deftly use CapCut Pro to craft Instagram Reels for the lab and scroll TikTok using a VPN (since it's banned on the University of Texas at Austin campus). He sees the future unfolding right before him. Corina isn't sitting around waiting for Hollywood to represent her. She's creating her own content and building a digital community on her own terms. She follows and engages with Latina TikTokers like Savannah Rivera (@savxrivera) and Filipina Latinas like Angelina Jacob (@yinyangelina), who unapologetically center ethnic joy, humor, language, and pride.

And Corina is far from alone. Many of Frederick's students who work at his Latinx Pop Lab at the University of Texas at Austin are doing the same—sidestepping outdated Nielsen metrics and Netflix's algorithmic tunnel vision as they actively seek out community-curated, identity-affirming, and culturally specific digital spaces that speak directly to their lives.

Peter observes how his sons, both now college graduates, curate their own media experiences through social platforms. They've gone beyond the algorithms of commercial streaming to start to find creators on YouTube or podcasts that give them the sense of community and culture they want, without it being fed to them. They've built networks of content creators who speak directly to their experiences as young Latinx men navigating professional worlds. This self-directed media consumption reveals how outdated industry assumptions about audiences have become.

Early Lessons

Peter's first show, *Greetings from Tucson*, which aired on The WB from September 2002 to May 2003, provided early lessons in the gap between real and ideal audiences. As he recalls, "I had Lupe Ontiveros playing the role of my grandma. I had Teri Garr and Martin Mull playing my Irish grandparents. I had Carmen Electra on it, and Vince Neil in a weird, crazy WB crossover thing. I had my pal, Jeff Garlin. I met Jacob Vargas, who I've worked with twice since, and will always work with. He's so amazing. Aimee Garcia got her start in *Greetings from Tucson*. It was a thrilling time."

The show represented something groundbreaking—a full season order for a series with six Latinx series regulars. When a WB casting executive called to remind all shows to be diverse in their casting, Peter's response revealed the absurdity of one-size-fits-all diversity mandates: "I told her how I had six series regulars that are Latin, and one white lady. So, I asked her if I should put more white people in the show. She laughed."

The timing was significant. *Greetings from Tucson* premiered the same year as *George Lopez*, creating what should have been a watershed moment for Latinx representation. At the American Latino Media Arts (ALMA) Awards that year, when Peter received a Producer of the Year award, George Lopez had just gotten his back-nine order. Rather than seeing competition, Peter saw collective progress: "When I got up to give my thank you speech at the ALMA Awards, the first thing I did was give a special acknowledgment to George. He was at the table, and people said he got a little tense, thinking that I'd go after him or something. I remember saying, 'George got his back nine. And when one of us wins, we all win. That's what we've got to keep doing.' This was a special time for me."

Yet despite the quality and groundbreaking nature of *Greetings from Tucson*, it lasted only one season. The show had found its real audience—Latinx families hungry for authentic representation—but couldn't convince network executives that this audience was valuable enough to sustain.

But even as digital platforms promise democratization, new pressures emerge—ones that often fall hardest on creators of color. Latinx content creators, in particular, find themselves navigating what we call the authenticity trap: the expectation to perform identity so as to satisfy both in-group expectations and out-group curiosity. It's a tightrope act. Too Mexican, and you risk alienating Central American viewers. Too urban, and you lose rural resonance. Too political, and brand sponsorships dry up. Not political enough, and you're accused of selling out.

Consider the bind facing Afro-Latina creators who build followings with candid videos about anti-Blackness in Latinx communities, only to be told by some viewers that they aren't "Latina enough" and by others that they're "too radical." Or queer Chicana creators whose work moves between drag performance and social commentary, and who report being shadow-banned or demonetized for discussing reproductive rights and gender fluidity in Spanish. These creators walk a cultural tightrope daily, shaping content that affirms identity while managing surveillance that is algorithmic, social, and commercial.

Frederick sees similar dynamics in academia, where Latinx scholars are expected to study their own communities (*authentic*) but to do so using white, Eurocentric scholarly frameworks (*legitimate*). The real audience—our communities—need grounded, accessible research on health disparities, education inequity, and cultural representation. But tenure committees often reward only work that passes through the filter of Derrida, Foucault, or Bourdieu. This is the double bind: Be authentic, but only in ways legible to institutions shaped by whiteness. The result? Exhaustion. Disillusionment. Or a compromise that never quite satisfies either audience.

Peter encounters it in nearly every writers' room. He's expected to be the cultural translator, the voice of all Latinx experience. "Would a Mexican mom really say that?" someone asks, as though there is one standard Latina *mamá* vernacular. "Is this authentic?" they press, as though authenticity were a singular, fixed category instead of a living, plural, evolving expression. These questions, however well-intentioned, reveal a deeper problem: The industry still imagines the Latinx audience as monolithic. It cannot yet accommodate the reality that Latinx stories span race, region, generation, class, language, and sexuality—sometimes all in a single household.

Aesopian Doublespeak

Both of us have learned to code-switch not only linguistically but also narratively—as a strategy for survival, yes, but also as a tool of subversion. Frederick can deploy narrative theory with the best of them, dropping Shklovsky, Genette, Todorov, Barthes, and Kristeva in one breath, then pivoting to *dichos* and childhood anecdotes in the next. Peter can talk "four-quadrant appeal" and "audience segmentation" in a pitch meeting, then write a scene later that night grounded in Spanglish, Tucson regional slang, and the cadence of his *tío*'s storytelling voice.

This code-switching often takes the form of what Frederick calls Aesopian doublespeak, a narrative strategy inspired by Aesop's animal fables, which used allegory to evade censors and smuggle subversive critiques of power into the audience's imagination. We see the same

Figure 7 *Reservation Dogs* (2021–2023) features four main protagonists (Wilhelmina Jacqueline "Willie Jack" Sampson, Bear Smallhill, Chester "Cheese" Williams, and Elora Danan Postoak), played by Indigenous actors (Paulina Alexis, Lane Factor, and Devery Jacobs).

strategy at work in contemporary Latinx- and Black, Indigenous, and People of Color-crafted narratives—stories that appear legible and acceptable to dominant-culture gatekeepers while embedding deeper layers of meaning, humor, and resistance for their real audiences. It's Gloria Anzaldúa's "*Haciendo caras*" or "Making face" with our communities, telling our stories truthfully while simultaneously resisting oppression through that storytelling. It's the hidden wink, the unspoken resonance, the line that seems innocuous to some but carries sacred weight for others. The "official" version gets you in the room; the layered version builds community.

We both see this brilliantly executed in Sterlin Harjo and Taika Waititi's *Reservation Dogs* (2021–2023). On the surface, it's a coming-of-age comedy about Indigenous teens in rural Oklahoma—a series anyone can enjoy. But for Native viewers, it's something more: a cultural ecosystem packed with inside jokes, kinship practices, spiritual humor, and intergenerational storytelling that refuses to translate itself. It's not just "representation"; it's reclamation. The show never stops to explain itself to outsiders. It trusts its core audience to understand, and it trusts outsiders to catch up.

This kind of layered storytelling is increasingly visible in the work of Latinx creators as well. We see it in Tanya Saracho's *Vida* (2018–

2020), where Spanglish isn't subtitled, gentrification isn't simplified, and the Latina gaze is celebrated: what Beltrán talks about as storytelling that privileges Latina perspectives, counters misrepresentation, and centers complicated, flawed Latina protagonists who refuse to soften their edges for mainstream comfort. We see it in Julio Torres's surrealist TV series, *Fantasmas* (2024), that bends genre and expectation while centering queer Salvadoran identity. These works do not beg for validation; they offer worlds. They model a future where Latinx creators don't just survive authenticity traps or rely on code-switching—they redefine the standards entirely.

Dollar-Sign Reality Checks

The white-optic media-industrial complex's fixation on ideal, universal audiences is aesthetic—and economic: Advertising rates, streaming deals, and international distribution hinge on delivering the "right" viewers. But as we have already begun to discuss, who gets to define what makes a viewer right? As always, it's the same entrenched systems that have historically devalued communities of color and continue to undercount our economic power today.

Consider this: Latinx purchasing power hit $1.9 trillion in 2020—a staggering number that continues to grow. Our children are among the many other new-generation Latinx that form the fastest-growing and most digitally engaged demographic in the United States. We overindex on media consumption, streaming, and social media interaction. The economic profiteering from our majority minority demographics does little to curtail what Molina-Guzmán, drawing on Dávila's "Latino spin," calls our "continued cultural and political invisibility."

Peter has argued with industry executives, until blue in the face, that their representation-demographic-profit equations don't make sense. They remain unmovable, fixed to this notion of the ideal audience as white or white-adjacent. As a result, Peter has watched promising projects with loyal Latinx audiences collapse because advertisers refused to pay premium rates. A show might reach millions of engaged viewers—but if those viewers don't align with white-centered industry expectations, the project is considered niche and not worth investing in. The logic is circular and brutal: Latinx-led shows get smaller budgets due to perceived market limits, then get canceled for not achieving the reach that those limited budgets can't sustain.

This isn't just a problem for new shows. Even *established* series with strong Latinx followings suffer from economic neglect. Tanya Saracho's critically acclaimed *Vida* (2018–2020) ran for just three seasons on STARZ, despite a devoted audience and numerous awards. We already mentioned that Gloria Calderón Kellett's *One Day at a Time,* a show Peter worked on, was canceled first by Netflix and then by Pop TV, even though it was beloved by critics and had a loyal and abundant Latinx fan base. These cancellations weren't driven by audience disinterest; they were driven by ad metrics and revenue models that never accounted for how and where Latinx viewers show up—often communally via shared logins or in off-platform discussions that don't get counted by engagement algorithms.

Fandoms

And yet, sometimes the real audience forces its way into the frame so powerfully that the industry can't ignore it.

Take *The Walking Dead* (2010–2022). The series became a cultural juggernaut in part because of the Latinx viewership that executives didn't initially court or expect. Characters like Rosita Espinosa (Christian Serratos) weren't central in early seasons. But the overwhelming fan response—especially from Latinx audiences—helped elevate Rosita to a series regular and key survivor. What happened behind the scenes was just as important as what happened on screen.

Frederick's current research into Latinx fandoms led to a compelling discovery: On fan forums, social media threads, and Tumblr pages dedicated to *The Walking Dead,* Latinx fans were reshaping the narrative landscape. While mainstream coverage fixated on Rick or Daryl, Latinx fans wrote expansive fanfic exploring Rosita's backstory, created fan art highlighting her resilience and tactical brilliance, and launched campaigns for increased screen time and character development. In essence, the real audience rewrote the show's priorities through sheer force of engagement.

This kind of fan-driven narrative correction is not unique to *The Walking Dead.* A similar phenomenon occurred with *Cobra Kai* (2018–

2025), where Latinx fans turned Miguel Diaz (Xolo Maridueña) into a breakout character. While the early seasons of the show continued to center Johnny Lawrence and Daniel LaRusso, fan enthusiasm for Miguel—his Ecuadorian roots, his bicultural identity, his moral complexity—helped shift the show's emotional center. Latinx fans didn't just consume; they contributed, reshaped, and reimagined.

We see this pattern across other white-optic storyworlds: in the rise of America Chavez fandoms despite her underdevelopment in the Marvel Cinematic Universe; in the Latinx-led commentary and remixes of *Stranger Things* (2016–2025) that center characters like Argyle (Eduardo Franco) as stoner-savior archetypes; and in Spanish-language memes that recontextualize *Euphoria*'s (2019–) Rue and Maddy in *quinceañera* aesthetics. Latinx fans are the *real* ideal audiences—and not as passive consumers, but as active co-creators. They reclaim characters. They resist narrative marginalization.

Nothing exposes the gulf between real and ideal audiences quite like the industry's persistent fear of Spanish. Peter has fought some version of the same battle in nearly every writers' room: even a line or two of Spanish is flagged as a risk. Executives worry the so-called ideal audience—white, monolingual, middle-class—will feel excluded or confused. This anxiety isn't about clarity; it's about control. It presumes the audience's incapacity rather than its adaptability.

And yet, real audiences code-switch daily. Our students fluidly move between English, Spanish, and Spanglish—not as performance, but as survival. They speak in a language shaped by migration, memory, region, and rhythm. What terrifies executives feels entirely ordinary to millions of people across the United States.

When *Jane the Virgin* premiered on The CW in 2014, it quietly revolutionized network TV by allowing characters to speak Spanish naturally—without apology and without explanation. And guess what? The audience kept up just fine. Likewise, Netflix's *Narcos* (2015–2017), despite its many representational shortcomings, featured long stretches of Spanish with English subtitles—and it became a global hit. The myth that audiences won't watch bilingual or subtitled content has been disproved again and again.

Even earlier, Robert Rodriguez refused to treat Spanish as secondary. In *El Mariachi* (1992), *Desperado* (1995), *Spy Kids* (2001),

Figure 8 Gina Rodriguez unapologetically speaks Spanish without subtitles as the titular Jane Gloriana Villanueva in *Jane the Virgin* (2014–2019).

and *Machete* (2010), Rodriguez created bilingual storyworlds that didn't translate culture for white comfort—they celebrated it. As Frederick explores in his book *The Cinema of Robert Rodriguez,* Rodriguez's so-called guerrilla aesthetic resists white-optic sanitization. He uses the language of film not as a barrier but as a portal—a means of inviting audiences into layered cultural spaces rather than flattening them into stereotypes.

Intergenerational Negotiations

But even among Latinx audiences, relationships to language and representation are complex—and often generational. Frederick's late *mamá* came of age watching screens filled with stereotypes: Desi Arnaz as the charming Latin lover, Charlton Heston in brownface as Ramon Miguel "Mike" Vargas in *Touch of Evil* (1958), and Rita Moreno as the fiery Anita in *West Side Story* (1961)—the lone Latina in a brownface cast. Had she lived to see Moreno return as Valentina in Spielberg's 2021 adaptation—alongside Rachel Zegler as Maria, Ariana DeBose as Anita, and David Alvarez as Bernardo—she would have wept. Not only for the casting, but for Moreno's second act as the wise *abuelita* in *One Day at a Time,* where she spoke Spanish, danced, cursed, and counseled with full dignity.

Peter sees this intergenerational negotiation play out in writers' rooms. Older Latinx writers, shaped by an era of assimilationist survival, often advocate broader, less culturally specific comedy. Younger writers—especially Latinas and LGBTQ+ creators—demand sharper nuance, intersectionality, and refusal. These differences aren't simply stylistic. They represent different strategies of endurance. One group learned to survive by being legible to whiteness; the other insists on being legible to themselves.

These tensions also surface in living rooms across the country. Latinx families debate shows like *Gentefied*—are the characters "too assimilated" or "too hood"? *In the Heights* (2021) sparked intense conversation about casting, colorism, and the dark Afro-Latinx absence in a supposedly Washington Heights–centered narrative. These aren't just debates about aesthetics; they are debates about belonging, memory, and cultural fidelity. The real audience isn't monolithic—it's in constant dialogue with itself.

Getting It Done

The gap between real and ideal audiences won't be closed by better algorithms or one-off inclusion initiatives—though both could help. What's needed is structural transformation: Latinx creatives not just present in writers' rooms but leading them. Not just featured on screen, but shaping narratives behind the camera. Not just brought into meetings, but running studios. As Frederick insists in *Latinx TV in the Twenty-First Century*, "We can't wait around for non-Latinxs to change the televisual order of things."

Robert Rodriguez used the money he earned from Paramount Pictures' *Desperado* (1995) to bankroll the creation of his own production house, Troublemaker Studios, in Austin, Texas. He founded it to maintain full creative control over his work and to craft a cinematic language that was fast, fiercely independent, unapologetically local, and proudly bicultural. From *El Mariachi* to *Spy Kids* to *Machete*, Rodriguez demonstrated that stories rooted in Latinx experience could be both commercially successful and culturally uncompromising. His do-it-yourself ethos and narrative boldness continue to inspire a new generation of Latinx filmmakers committed to writing, directing, and producing on their own terms.

Following this blueprint for autonomy and cultural integrity within the brown-optic televisual narrative spaces, as early as 2005, Eva Longoria, long a vocal advocate for Latinx visibility in media, launched UnbeliEVAble Entertainment to center authentic, complex portrayals of Latinx lives on screen. Recognizing that representation and civic engagement go hand in hand, Longoria partnered more recently with America Ferrera to co-found She Se Puede (2020), a digital platform and community designed to empower Latinas through storytelling, organizing, and political education. Also in 2020, we saw Tanya Saracho launch Ojalá Productions to carve space for queer, feminist Latinx storytelling: stories that push past the boundaries of palatable representation and instead thrive in their specificity and political sharpness. And around this time, Gloria Calderón Kellett built GloNation Studios to develop Latinx serialized stories like *With Love* (2021–2023), extending the multigenerational, bilingual, intersectional *familia* storytelling she pioneered on *One Day at a Time*—shows that refuse to flatten identities. By building their own production companies, they're bypassing outdated industry assumptions and shifting the center of creative power. Their work insists that Latinx stories are not side dishes—they're the main course.

Peter sees the shift firsthand in actors launching production companies, writers tired of watering down their work, and directors refusing to wait for market validation. They aren't asking for permission. They're building storyworlds where cultural specificity isn't a liability, it's the point. This is what attracted Peter to working with the comic book publisher Ignition Press on his new Latinx futurist miniseries, *TEQ*.

Eyes-Wide-Open Critical Optimism

Despite the frustrations, we remain cautiously optimistic. Not because the industry has suddenly awakened to Latinx brilliance. It hasn't. Not because the algorithms have somehow shed their bias—they haven't. But because the real audience has become undeniable. Every year, more creators tell specific, culturally grounded stories. Every year, those stories find their people. Every year, the myth of the "universal viewer" becomes harder to defend.

Frederick's students are part of that shift. They critique media with sharp, intersectional lenses—but they also generate their own content: fanfic, TikToks, Vimeo shorts, comics, and tweet-sized micronarratives. What's striking is how these students never wait for validation from the industry. They write themselves into storyworlds without apology, building narrative communities that reflect their hybrid identities and complex realities.

We also take heart in shows—yes, even those prematurely canceled—that dared to trust their audiences. *Vida* offered queer, feminist Latinx storytelling that refused to translate itself. *Mr. Iglesias* embraced bilingual, working-class humor from a teacher's point of view. *Gentefied*, *Cristela*, *One Day at a Time*—each told stories rooted in specificity, region, language, and love. Even when these shows were pulled from streaming or cut short by executives, they seeded something lasting: a refusal to compromise identity for market legibility.

One of the more recent and resonant examples is Shea Serrano's *Primo* (2023), with Peter as a contributing writer on episode 3, "The Ride Home." Set in the Latinx-majority city of San Antonio—just an hour south of Frederick in Austin—the semiautobiographical show centers a Mexican American teen raised by his single mom and five uncles, each wildly different and hilariously devoted. *Primo* doesn't rely on trauma or caricature; instead, it finds its humor and heart in the ordinary, everyday chaos of the lives of a working-class familia. The show trusts its audience to understand the rhythms of Spanglish, the significance of H-E-B references, and the deep cultural specificity of growing up brown in South Texas. This storytelling confidence, leaning deeply into cultural specificity, marks a shift, at least for us, from performative representation to lived-in storytelling. It's what Beltrán calls "cultural sincerity": storytelling that is "*sincere to a creator's vision and community*," not politically cor-

Figure 9 Amazon Freevee's *Primo* (2023) portrays Latinx everyday life as the norm, rather than an anomaly.

rect facsimile. This is precisely what makes these shows resonate. As such, it naturally refuses to flatten Latinx experience for palatability, nor does it burden itself with proving its worth. It just tells a brown, South Texas story.

Beyond Latinx-centered content, we're also seeing non-white-optic shows break through. *Abbott Elementary* (2021–) centers Black public school teachers in Philadelphia with warmth and wit, never asking the audience to decode or universalize Blackness. *Reservation Dogs* masterfully immerses us in the lives of Muscogee (Creek) Nation teens in rural Oklahoma—without ever pausing to explain kinship structures, inside jokes, or spiritual references to outsiders. Likewise, *Ramy* (2019–2022) explores Muslim American identity with specificity, contradiction, and complexity; *Mo* (2022–2025), created by Ramy Youssef and Mo Amer, offers Palestinian Houstonite perspectives rarely seen on screen, delivered in English, Spanish, and Arabic.

These shows work not because they universalize (i.e., dilute) identity, but because they deepen it. They don't center the so-called ideal viewer. They speak from the inside out—and so expand the storyworlds we all get to live in.

Brown-Optic Audiences

Every creative decision, from casting to dialogue to storyline, implies an audience. When we subtitle Spanish, we imagine viewers who need help. When we don't, we trust them to keep up. When we explain cultural practices, we center outsiders. When we simply show them, we center insiders. This is the making of what Frederick calls in *Latinx TV in the Twenty-First Century* brown oculi narratives that bring "great will to style" with deep responsibility to cultural authenticity and the ability to "smuggle in decolonial modes of thinking, feeling, and behaving."

The white-optic media-industrial complex still chases its ideal audience—white, middle-class, monolingual, algorithm-approved—but the cracks in that foundation widen daily. Streaming may have disappointed in some ways, but it has also revealed the hunger for stories that broadcast never dared to feed. Social media may have introduced new anxieties, but it has proven that specificity travels. A joke for your *primos* can go viral because somewhere, someone sees themselves in it. It's not universality that makes content resonate; it's resonance that makes it universal.

We write for the real audience—complex, multilingual, multigenerational, critical, and loving. They don't need us to be perfect or palatable. They need us to be honest. They need us to tell stories that reflect the full, messy, joyful, painful reality of Latinx life without apology or translation.

Frederick has always written toward this audience. In his scholarship, he maps the cultural, political, and visual grammar of Latinx popular cultural narratives. In his children's books and young adult fiction, such as *Con Papá / With Papá* (2022) and *The Absolutely (Almost) True Adventures of Max Rodriguez* (2024), he invites young bilingual, nonbinary Latinx readers to see themselves as protagonists, creators, and cultural translators in their own right. In his comic book *Pyroclast* (2023) and graphic novels *Through Fences* (2024) and *Labyrinths Borne* (2024), for instance, he crafts vibrant, emotionally complex Latinx characters who don't explain themselves to the reader. They exist, with full cultural density and affective truth.

Peter does the same through screenplays, comics, and his historical fiction, *Blood and Gold: The Legend of Joaquin Murrieta* (2021), creating layered narratives that speak to queer, brown, working-class life without diluting or flattening it. His scripts resist industry pressure to universalize trauma or explain identity. In his comics, he writes for insiders—the *tías* and *tíos* who know the rhythm of Spanglish, the feel of silence at the dinner table, the push-pull of assimilation and resistance. His work trusts the reader to recognize what matters, even if it's never footnoted or decoded.

Latinx creatives like us craft stories for audiences who have always been here, always listening—audiences who don't just consume but co-create meaning. Audiences who write fanfic, remix scenes, argue on group chats, and teach our work in classrooms we never imagined reaching. Audiences who are real, not because of metrics, but because of their engagement, their memory, and their presence.

Chapter 3

LATINX NARCO NARRATIVES AND THE NEO-WESTERN

In his Latinx Pop Culture course, Frederick teaches a unit titled "The Narco Imaginary." On the first day of this section, he asks students to close their eyes and take mental notes of what they visualize when they hear the phrase *drug dealer*. The responses are nearly always the same: brown skin, facial tattoos, gold chains, guns, urban decay, or desert landscapes scorched and empty. Then he asks them to picture a pharmaceutical executive. Suddenly, the descriptors shift: white, clean-cut, suited, suburban. Both push addictive substances. Both profit from human suffering. But only one becomes the villain in the white-optic media-industrial complex's spinning of narrative webs that shape the nation's collective imagination.

This is where we begin our exploration of narco narratives and the neo-Western: with the racialized imagery burned into American consciousness through decades of visual repetition and ideological reinforcement. Jason Ruiz traces this pattern, with its deep historical roots, as one that persistently links Latin American immigrants and latinidad to drug-related crime and violence across what he calls "narcomedia." The desert—that vast in-between space coded as simultaneously empty and dangerous—becomes the moral and aesthetic battleground where white America projects its fears of brownness, lawlessness, and the breakdown of empire. It's no accident that so many narco-centered stories are staged here. The desert is never neutral. It's loaded, mythic, and violent—an iconic set piece of settler-colonial anxiety.

Peter knows these landscapes intimately. As professor of practice and Deputy Director at The Sidney Poitier New American Film School at Arizona State University, he works and teaches in the heart of the Sonoran Desert. His students—many of them first-generation, Latinx, Native American, and working-class—are reclaiming this terrain not as backdrop, but as living space, community, and memory. They film in barrios and borderlands they call home, flipping the Western trope on its head. Yet even as they do this work, Peter has observed how quickly white-optic media swoop in to reinscribe old hierarchies. Hollywood crews descend from L.A., shoot poverty and trauma for aesthetic texture, hole up in air-conditioned hotels, and fly back—never engaging meaningfully with the communities they depict.

This extractive visual practice reinforces a kind of narco-tourism: white-optic-constructed stories about Latinx people, but never for them. Crews want the "authentic" look—dust, desperation, danger—but they rarely hire local creatives to shape the narrative. Local fixers, often the only Latinx people with real on-set power, become intermediaries between white directors chasing "grit" and neighborhoods tired of being reduced to criminal spectacle. These fixers carry the emotional labor of translation, damage control, and cultural accuracy—tasks uncredited in the final cut.

Frederick's books on Latinx media and visual culture focus precisely on this, aiming to make visible how this white optic shapes narco tropes that travel back and forth from *Breaking Bad* (2008–2013), *Narcos* (2015–2017), and *Coyote* (2021) to mainstream films like *Scarface* (1983), *Traffic* (2000), *Savages* (2012), *Sicario* (2015) and *Sicario: Day of the Soldado* (2018), and *Griselda* (2024) shape the mainstream audiences' binary logic of brown equals desert-as-chaos versus white equals suburb-as-civilization.

Peter has the same goal as seen in his screen work. In scripts and fiction, he rewrites the brown inhabited desert not as a lawless wasteland but as a repository of collective memory and defiant survival. His characters don't exist to be hunted or reformed—they claim the landscape as theirs, pushing back against the cinematic language that made their existence seem aberrant in the first place.

The white-optic-constructed narco imaginary collapses complexity. It erases structural violence—poverty, policing, foreign policy, racial capitalism—in favor of character pathology. It trades in spectacle over substance. And in doing so, it turns the real-world consequences of empire and extraction into aestheticized trauma porn. However, in both pedagogy and practice, Latinx scholars and creatives like us demand a different kind of storytelling—one rooted in lived geography, political clarity, and narrative sovereignty. As our students know, the desert doesn't need to be rewritten as something else. It needs to be reclaimed on its own terms, not as mythic void but as ancestral territory, not as chaos but as contested homeland.

Neocolonial Alchemies

Breaking Bad perfected the formula: A white man enters brown-inhabited landscapes, masters brown economies, and transcends brown limitations. Walter White doesn't just cook meth; he colonizes an entire illicit economy, displacing Latino players through superior chemistry, business acumen, and brutal efficiency. The show frames his arc as a tragic moral descent, but structurally, it's a story of neocolonial domination. It's *manifest destiny* in a hazmat suit.

Consider the character trajectory: Walter first buys from Krazy-8—a stereotypical gateway Latino dealer, disposable and thinly developed. He moves on to Tuco Salamanca: volatile, hyperviolent, unpredictable, brownness reduced to threat. From there, he eclipses them all. Gustavo Fring, a more complex figure—Chilean, queer-coded, disciplined—initially appears to break the mold. But even he is ultimately a stepping-stone. Gus is killed not because he fails, but because he succeeds too well within a system never meant for him to win. His downfall reinforces the show's underlying message: The Latino drug trade exists as something to be appropriated, outsmarted, and ultimately *transcended* by white male ambition.

Even in criminality, we are positioned as the local color, the chaotic threat, the cultural wallpaper. The brown bodies and border economies are not explored in terms of their origin or context—they are absorbed into a white character's narrative of agency and self-actualization.

We've often discussed how our students, especially film and media majors, defend the show's artistic excellence—and we don't disagree. *Breaking Bad* is formally masterful. Its cinematography is stunning, its performances compelling, its writing sharp and layered. But formal brilliance does not absolve ideological violence. Good art can still reproduce bad ideas. And in this case, the show's visual inventiveness makes its cultural appropriation all the more insidious.

When Frederick teaches the episode "Negro y Azul," students begin to see this more clearly. The cold open features a narco-corrido—stylized, stylized, stylized—about Heisenberg's legend growing in Mexico. Sung in Spanish, the scene plays like a parody or pastiche, signaling "authenticity" while draining the corrido tradition of its historical and political charge. The narco-corrido, long used by border communities to document resistance, violence, and state collusion, becomes, in the hands of *Breaking Bad*, mere exotic flavor. It sets the tone not to elevate Mexican agency, but to mythologize the white outlaw.

This is an act of narrative alchemy—the transformation of Latinx suffering, tradition, and presence into symbolic fuel for white-centered storytelling. It's a kind of cultural laundering: Our stories get cleaned, sharpened, rebranded, and sold back to mass audiences without the messiness of our actual lives, voices, or politics.

But we teach this not to dismiss *Breaking Bad*, but to dissect it, so that our students can learn to recognize how visual mastery and narrative harm can coexist. We want them to be able to distinguish between representation and repossession. To ask not just "Is this good?" but "Good for whom? And at what cost?"

The Salamanca Problem

The Salamanca family encapsulates everything broken about Latinx representation in the neo-Western. Tuco is pure id—violence without motivation, rage without reason. His presence signals chaos rather than character. Hector Salamanca, reduced to a bell-ringing invalid, becomes a literal metaphor for voicelessness—he cannot speak for himself, and his agency is stripped away in both form and function. The cousins, Leonel and Marco, are mute, stylized assassins: slow-motion specters whose silence codes them as prelinguistic, premodern—less than human, more than threat.

Only Lalo, introduced later in *Better Call Saul* (2015–2022), breaks the mold with charisma, intelligence, and tactical savvy. But even Lalo is framed as a *charming psychopath* rather than a *complex person*—a Hannibal Lecter in cowboy boots, dangerous not because of his violence, but because of how enjoyable it is to watch him perform it. He is an upgrade in writing, but still a variation on the same theme: Latinx men as spectacular, stylish criminals who exist to heighten the narrative stakes of white or white-coded protagonists.

Peter has pitched dozens of Latinx characters across networks and development rooms, and the Salamanca specter looms large. Executives reference them constantly: "Like Tuco but more sympathetic," "Like the cousins, but with lines." The *Breaking Bad* franchise didn't just succeed—it created a representational template. Latinx characters in crime narratives now enter a binary: either replicate the Salamanca mold (familiar evil) or exist in explicit contrast to it (narrative counterpoint). Both options still orbit the same stereotype.

The deeper irony is that real-world border economies and narco networks are often highly sophisticated: structured hierarchies, strict logistics, political entanglements, and even intergenerational strategy. These organizations behave more like multinational corporations than chaotic gangs. Yet *Breaking Bad* and its derivatives code Latinx criminality as primitive, reactive, and emotionally unstable—disorganized crime contrasted with Walter White's cold, calculated enterprise. His meth is pure because he is a chemist. Theirs is impure because . . . they are Latinx. The subtext is clear: Whiteness equals precision and genius; brownness equals chaos and failure.

Figure 10 Raymond Cruz plays Tuco, one of *Breaking Bad*'s (2008–2013) most memorable antagonists.

Lateral Moves

Better Call Saul promised to offer more textured portrayals of its Latinx characters—and in some ways, it delivered. It spends more time in Latinx spaces, gives characters like Nacho Varga inner lives, and offers glimpses of dignity in otherwise brutalizing contexts. Michael Mando brings deep vulnerability and charisma to Nacho, making him one of the most emotionally compelling characters in the franchise. But ultimately, *Better Call Saul* reinforces the same racialized dynamics: white characters—Jimmy, Mike, Gus—are allowed complexity, contradiction, and moral elasticity. Latinx characters remain reactionary: They respond to violence but rarely get to reframe its logic.

Nacho's arc is particularly frustrating. He's caught in a vise: a son trying to protect his father's legitimate upholstery business while trapped in a blood-soaked underworld run by the Salamancas. His choices are impossible, not because he lacks character, but because the writing offers him no narrative escape. He cannot pivot, outsmart, or reinvent. His fate is sealed from the outset. His death is brutal, poetic even, but it serves the emotional development of other characters, not the fulfillment of his own arc.

Frederick uses Nacho's story in class to discuss ideas of narrative determinism, such as how Latinx characters in prestige crime TV are born into tragedy with no viable off-ramps. White characters like Walter and Jesse *choose* crime—they dabble, ascend, fall. Their arcs are shaped by agency and consequence. Latinx characters like Nacho are written into crime—as if it were inherited, environmental, or inevitable. This naturalization of Latinx criminality—crime as fate, not decision—reinforces damaging real-world ideologies about culture, biology, and moral capacity.

What both *Breaking Bad* and *Better Call Saul* share is a refusal to imagine Latinx characters outside of narco contexts. They are narratively useful but rarely narratively central. They carry narrative weight but are denied narrative sovereignty.

And that's the Salamanca problem: not just that these characters are violent, but that violence is the only language they're ever allowed to speak.

Neocolonial Optics

Netflix's *Narcos* (2015–2017) cloaks itself in the aesthetics of prestige realism, complete with faux-documentary narration, archival footage, and immersive production design. But beneath this high production gloss lies a deep structural bias—one that reasserts colonial hierarchies under the guise of global storytelling. The white Drug Enforcement Agency narrator doesn't just guide us through the plot; he frames the story, reinscribing the colonial gaze as epistemologically necessary. The audience sees Colombia not through its own eyes but through the filtered consciousness of U.S. drug enforcement. History becomes a white interior monologue.

The use of bilingual dialogue at first seems progressive, until you notice the rules: Spanish is relegated to moments of anger, violence, and color, while English is used to explain plot and deliver "serious" dialogue. The linguistic code-switching mirrors the cultural one: Spanish signifies exoticism and irrationality; English denotes authority and clarity. For Spanish-speaking viewers, this hierarchy is glaring—and grating. It's not just what language is spoken, but *when, by whom,* and *for what purpose.*

By centering Pablo Escobar, the show performs a mythologizing gesture that renders Latin American narco economies as natural outgrowths of individual pathology. Escobar becomes both folk hero and supervillain—a stand-in for all Colombian crime. The political context—Cold War interventions, International Monetary Fund restructuring, agricultural collapse—is stripped away in favor of baroque violence and spectacle. As Frederick often notes in his classes, this isn't so different from the way Old Hollywood turned Pancho Villa into a caricature of Mexican revolution. It's historical déjà vu.

Peter's failed narco project is telling. It reveals the narrow bandwidth of acceptable Latinx storytelling within the industry. The rejection of scripts focused on economic policy, rural displacement, and human costs in favor of gunfights and vengeance arcs points to a deeper fear: nuance doesn't sell. Complexity humanizes. Humanization of Latinx characters remains a risk that networks are reluctant to take.

Economics of White Dominance

Ozark (2017–2022) presents itself as a character study of moral collapse, but its racial politics are deeply insidious. The Byrdes are presented as reluctant but ultimately superior participants in the drug trade—wily enough to survive, clever enough to innovate, and emotionally distant enough to rationalize everything. Their whiteness is never named but always operative. It is the unspoken passport that grants them access to systems of power—banks, politics, law enforcement—that are sealed off to brown characters.

The Navarro cartel, in contrast, remains mostly faceless, exoticized, and trope laden. Despite being multinational criminal moguls, they need Marty Byrde to "solve" their money laundering problems. This reproduces a colonial logic: Latinx people have wealth and power but lack institutional sophistication. They can accumulate capital, but not legitimacy. They can inspire fear but not respect.

Frederick uses *Ozark* in his media studies classrooms to map the psychogeography of whiteness: The show constructs a world where

Figure 11 Laura Linney and Jason Bateman star in *Ozark* (2017–2022) as money launderers Wendy and Marty Byrde.

every narrative turn confirms the superiority of white strategic thinking over brown chaos. Even the cartel's violence becomes a prop for Byrde family drama. The cartel exists not as a subject in its own right but as a crucible to test the Byrdes' emotional mettle.

And while *Ozark* nods at privilege—through characters like Ruth or Maya—it stops short of interrogating how race and class intertwine. The Byrdes are always in control of their narrative. Latinx characters are subject to it. They are cast as thresholds—obstacles, enablers, occasionally threats—but never narrative *centers*. In that way, *Ozark* extends the *Breaking Bad* tradition: White protagonists are granted moral ambiguity, while brown antagonists are rendered symbolically static.

Insider's Burden

Mayans M.C. (2018–2023) was born of a paradox: It sought to tell an insider's story within an outsider's structure. As a spinoff of *Sons of Anarchy* (2008–2014), the show inherited a genre saturated with white biker masculinity, toxic brotherhood, and hyperviolence. Co-creator Elgin James—a former gang member with African American, Dominican, and Irish heritage—brought authenticity to the project, but he also inherited a canon built around Anglo rebellion.

The result is a show that oscillates between resistance and repetition. Episodes weave in scenes of cultural specificity—border patrol raids, altar rituals, Nahuatl terms, generational trauma—but must always circle back to the crime arc. In other words, the show offers glimpses of narrative sovereignty but not control. It must entertain before it can educate.

Peter, in conversation with *Mayans* writers, learned how hard it is to sustain these interventions. They describe late-night arguments over how much Nahuatl to include, how many Indigenous references would be "too much" for the network, how to balance genre fidelity with cultural responsibility. Their labor is at once narrative, pedagogical, political, and emotional. The burden isn't just to write a good script. It's to justify the existence of brown stories in a white franchise.

The best moments of *Mayans M.C.*—those that explore deportation trauma, the prison-industrial complex, and multigenerational identity—point to what Latinx genre storytelling could be if unshackled from legacy constraints. But as Frederick often says, narrative sovereignty cannot be partial. It must be structural. Until then, shows such as *Mayans M.C.* operate in a state of narrative negotiation—necessary, powerful, but still provisional.

Regenerative Whiteness

If *Ozark* masks white supremacy behind financial prowess and *Mayans M.C.* negotiates cultural authenticity within white-inherited structures, *Coyote* (2021) lays bare the white-savior scaffolding with remarkable clarity—despite its stated intention to avoid it. Marketed by CBS (soon rebranded Paramount+) as a bold psychological drama set in the U.S.-Mexico borderlands, *Coyote* purports to upend the white-savior narrative. Instead, it recycles it under the guise of character transformation, centering Ben Clemens (Michael Chiklis), a retired Border Patrol agent who undergoes a moral awakening after being ensnared in the very migrant world he once policed.

The show performs a bait-and-switch: We are promised a "non-white-savior" story, only to watch six episodes of a white everyman's redemptive journey made possible through the suffering and humanity of brown characters. Clemens is repeatedly described in press materials as a man forced to reckon with his biases. Yet the narrative makes his transformation the central drama, while Mexican and Central American characters orbit as catalysts. Clemens's journey—symbolically hammered home through metaphors like rebuilding his deceased Immigration and Customs Enforcement partner's house—frames his moral growth as the ultimate arc. María Elena, a pregnant Salvadoran teen, functions less as an autonomous subject and more as a vessel for Clemens's newfound conscience.

Frederick talks about this dynamic as a form of white regeneration through brown suffering. This pattern—also exemplified in *Breaking Bad, Better Call Saul, Ozark,* and even *Cobra Kai*—allows white male protagonists to recover purpose, self-worth, and moral clarity by immersing themselves in brown worlds, then emerging transformed. The trope requires brown pain and dispossession as narrative fuel. In *Coyote,* this includes flashbacks of María Elena's trauma, reductive gender roles for Latinas (maids, mothers, domestic figures), and hypermasculine Latino archetypes (cartel henchmen, *puñal*-shouting tough guys).

Mayans M.C., in contrast, at least attempts to disrupt these tropes from within. Writers like Elgin James bring insider perspective and push to include Indigenous and Latinx specificity, even as they're constrained by the white-centered outlaw genre inherited from *Sons of Anarchy.* But *Coyote,* driven by white creative leadership, imposes white-centered morality over brown complexity. As Frederick argues in his essay, the series offers an Olympian god's view of the border, reducing it to a metaphorical terrain for white redemption—its toylike opening sequences literalizing the showrunners' manipulative gaze.

Meanwhile, musical cues in *Coyote* reinforce spatial and racial coding: Hip-hop-infused beats mark transitions into "Mexican" scenes, while English-language dialogue dominates all moments of moral reckoning. Even Native characters are rendered through dated Western tropes—desert trackers reduced to tools in Clemens's spiritual voyage. The show may profess to humanize brown folks, but its logic remains extractive: brownness as experience, white man as protagonist.

Peter encounters these tropes constantly in pitch meetings. Executives demand "relatable" white characters to carry Latinx stories, even when the setting, plot, and stakes clearly belong elsewhere. What results is a flood of shows in which whiteness is never named but always in control—privileged, resilient, and unburdened by structural critique.

Coyote underscores the central contradiction in white-regenerative televisual narratives: They claim to dismantle white heroism while doubling down on its aesthetic and emotional economy. For Frederick, this exemplifies how the televisual industrial complex continues to rope burn our Brown souls with these palatable illusions of racial progress. Shows like *Coyote* don't challenge the system; they rebrand it. For once, a show's cancellation felt like justice, not loss.

Western's Eternal Return and Aestheticized Fear

The Western never really died; it just changed clothes. In the neo-Western, the cowboy hat becomes a hazmat suit, the six-shooter becomes a sniper rifle, and the "savage Indian" becomes the "savage narco." The narrative logic persists: Brownness is danger, whiteness is order.

In a book Frederick co-authored with William Nericcio, *Talking #browntv: Latinas and Latinos on the Screen*, he dissects representations of Latinx in Cowboy-Western mythmaking at its roots. He traces how frontier narratives were never about the frontier; they were about white redemption. They justified conquest by staging whiteness as beleaguered, besieged, and morally triumphant. This template adapts easily to the border: The desert becomes the new frontier, the cartel the new Comanche. The moral structure doesn't change—only the villains do.

Even speculative shows like *The Mandalorian* (2019–2023) reproduce these tropes. Pedro Pascal's protagonist wears a helmet, flattening ethnicity into visual anonymity. The Tusken Raiders, coded as Indigenous, are still treated as obstacles to be managed. When they are "humanized," it's through the eyes of the white-coded protagonist. And when they are massacred, it is justified as part of the hero's quest. This is not representation. It is narrative containment.

Neo-Westerns rely on what Frederick calls "heroic extraction"—where the white protagonist enters brown space, extracts meaning, and exits morally tested but unchanged. It's a colonial adventure dressed in grit. The lesson for Latinx creators is not just to critique the Western, but to reimagine what story structures can look like without it.

Sicario (2015) is a masterclass in tension. Every shot is composed like a prayer, every scene choreographed for maximum dread. But

Figure 12 One of *Sicario*'s (2015) most iconic scenes takes place predominantly across the Ciudad Juárez-El Paso border.

what does this dread serve? The answer is not narrative complexity, it's ideological clarity. The border in *Sicario* is a nightmare so total that only extralegal violence can contain it. This is the logic of the drone strike, the black site, and the wall.

Emily Blunt's character is a cipher for the white liberal viewer: idealistic, procedural, ultimately impotent. She learns what *Sicario* wants you to learn—that order is an illusion and violence is necessary, but necessary for whom?

Benicio del Toro's Alejandro is the emotional lever that makes this logic work. His family was murdered by cartels, and now he murders with righteous fury. He is, as Frederick argues, a "license character"—a brown figure whose suffering authorizes the white viewer's bloodlust. His trauma isn't resolved; it is *instrumentalized.* Through him, *Sicario* argues that the only way to survive the border is to become what the border fears.

Peter has spoken with students from El Paso who watched *Sicario* with quiet fury. It is their hometown turned into a backdrop for someone else's catharsis. Their schools, homes, and parks are erased. Juárez becomes hell; El Paso becomes a waiting room for hell. This isn't just a distortion, it's a disappearance.

Tragic Latinas

Queen of the South (2016–2021) attempts a rare feat within narco storytelling: a feminist retelling of a genre built around masculinist violence. Teresa Mendoza's rise from a low-level money changer to a drug empire queen suggests female possibility in a space typically reserved for patriarchs—particularly among U.S. Latinas who saw in Teresa a model of resilience, ambition, and coded feminist defiance.

But while Teresa ascends the cartel hierarchy, she is forced to shed what Hollywood deems feminine: vulnerability, compassion, community. Unlike male antiheroes (Tony Soprano, Walter White, Marty Byrde), who maintain family ties and psychological nuance, Teresa must become hyperefficient, emotionally inert, and ruthlessly transactional to survive. Her character arc resembles not a liberation but a transformation into an instrument of the same patriarchal structures she ostensibly challenges.

We think here of Hugo Benavides's insights on the narco-drama, where Teresa's rise reads as an antipatriarchal "nonmasculine iconization" that nonetheless leaves the genre's patriarchal structure intact. What we see is gender inversion, not gender liberation: rather than authentic expression, the form compels Teresa to adopt male-coded ruthlessness.

Peter's experience as a consultant in the early stages of the series revealed the central dilemma: How do you script a powerful Latina lead inside structures—the narco-economy and Hollywood's own gender paradigms—that inherently deny her humanity? Writers' room discussions circled this double bind. When Teresa expresses emotion, she's seen as weak. When she suppresses it, she's accused of lacking dimension. The result is a character hailed as a feminist icon who, paradoxically, affirms the logic of male-coded violence as the only viable path to power. As feminist media scholars argue, real subversion requires more than flipping gendered roles—it requires challenging the values embedded in those roles.

Netflix's *Griselda* (2024), starring Sofía Vergara as the infamous Griselda Blanco, raises similar questions while amplifying the stakes. Billed as "inspired by a true story," the series leans into Blanco's real-life notoriety to dramatize her rise as the so-called Godmother of Cocaine. But instead of offering a complex deconstruction of narco power and gender, *Griselda* often revels in its subject's brutality.

The show aestheticizes violence under the guise of empowerment, creating what we've discussed as a cosmetic performance of Latina empowerment—where the Latina protagonist achieves power only by mimicking the hyperviolence of their male counterparts, with little interrogation of the systems that produce that violence.

Blanco is presented not just as a woman navigating a male-dominated world, but as one who masters its codes so thoroughly she surpasses her male rivals in ruthlessness. Yet we learn little about her internal world, her contradictions, or the human cost of her ambition. Her identity as a Colombian woman, mother, and immigrant is reduced to narrative texture rather than thematic core. In this way, *Griselda* risks becoming what it purports to critique: a glamorized account of cartel ascent that substitutes representation for transformation.

We consider Jacques Audiard's *Emilia Pérez* (2024) as offering a provocative counterpoint. Part crime thriller, part operatic musical, and part trans liberation narrative, the film centers on a notorious Mexican narco kingpin who undergoes gender transition and reinvents himself as Emilia Pérez, a woman seeking redemption through philanthropic work and maternal reconnection. Unlike *Queen of the South* or *Griselda*, *Emilia Pérez* dares to imagine transformation not as a rebranding of violence, but as a break from it.

In embracing musical numbers and emotional vulnerability, *Emilia Pérez* breaks with the realism of narco noir and instead embraces stylization as critique. However, while super innovative, we wrestle with the many questions it raises. Can a French director *and* a Spanish lead (trans actor Karla Sofía Gascón is from Spain) with no direct ties to the communities depicted and the traditions of white-optic narco narratives that have traditionally contained Mexico and Mexicans sidestep exoticization? And, in terms of the narrative proper, we ask: Can a former narco truly escape the world that forged them? Can gender transition serve as both a metaphor and a literal exit from patriarchal power?

Our verdict: While *Emilia Pérez* is undeniably innovative and offers moments of transformative empathy, it does so while reinscribing Eurocolonial and gendered tropes that limit the very humanity it seeks to affirm. It slips into white-optic tropes that undermine its radical potential.

To wit: Even after Emilia's transition, her character is frequently framed through stereotypical lenses—hyperemotional, explosively temperamental, and ultimately violent. Rather than fully escaping the hypermasculine codes of the narco genre, Emilia is pulled back into them—framed less as a woman navigating post-transition peace and more as a dangerous Latina whose rage simmers just beneath the surface. This perpetuates a long-standing cinematic pattern: representing trans and Latina bodies as volatile, excessive, and emotionally unstable.

The broader problem is that in both *Queen of the South* and *Griselda*, power is legible only through domination. These narratives don't ask what other forms power might take—collective, relational, restorative—but instead reassert that only through exceptional violence can women thrive in patriarchal systems. *Emilia Pérez*, by contrast, poses a different question: What if the path to power is also a path to peace? Yet its answer is compromised by the film's own reliance on tropes it fails to fully interrogate.

We constantly remind our students that true narrative disruption doesn't merely put Latinas at the top of violent hierarchies; it imagines worlds where those hierarchies are dismantled altogether. Until that happens, the narco queen remains a tragic figure—not because she seeks power, but because she must trade her humanity to achieve it.

Singing Hollywood's Silences

Where Hollywood trades in narco spectacle and moral binaries, narcocorridos offer narrative elasticity. The tradition of drug ballads in Mexican and Chicana/o communities operates less as glamorization than as vernacular journalism: documenting survival, grief, betrayal, and resilience amid systems that fail to protect or provide. These songs are often layered with ambiguity, blending critique with tribute, despair with dignity. Artists like Los Tigres del Norte, Chalino Sánchez, and Gerardo Ortiz do not sanitize; they narrate.

After having students read excerpts from Américo Paredes' *With His Pistol in His Hand* (1958), Frederick plays narco-corridos and screens Robert M. Young's *The Ballad of Gregorio Cortez* (1982) in class to showcase a deep-time borderland epistemology that challenges cinematic conventions. (The film remains one of the few American cinematic texts that takes the corrido form seriously.) Gregorio Cortez, a Tejano farmer, becomes a folk hero not through criminal ambition but through resistance: falsely accused, hunted across Texas, and immortalized in song. The corrido frames him not as a villain or saint, but as a man shaped by linguistic misunderstanding, racial violence, and cultural erasure. Young's film follows that logic, resisting Hollywood's impulse for resolution or white saviorism. The viewer is not granted moral clarity, only the chance to bear witness.

Frederick recalls how, when he first studied the film as an undergraduate at the University of California, Berkeley, in Mario Barrera's Introduction to Chicano Film class, it changed the way he thought about storytelling and sovereignty; how the corrido stood in for a silenced archive; and how Cortez became a symbol of narrative reclamation. It was the first time he had seen a film not just about Mexican American life but also structurally guided by its own traditions.

That experience informs how he has taught *The Ballad of Gregorio Cortez*: not as genre flavor, but as a formal counterhistory. For Frederick, Young's *The Ballad of Gregorio Cortez* is a cinematic corrido in its own right, foregrounding injustice and celebrating collective memory and community activism. It stands radically apart from those white-optic narco narratives like *Breaking Bad* that extract aesthetic cues (dusty landscapes, Catholic iconography, banda music) and strip them of context, and that isolate and atomize the antihero. The brown-shaped visuo-sonicscapes of something like *The Ballad of Gregorio Cortez* center the collective—the family, the barrio, the border community. It doesn't ask who is bad. It asks what circumstances forced these decisions.

Figure 13 Edward James Olmos brings folk hero Gregorio Cortez to life in this acclaimed "cinematic corrido."

There is a profound irony: The same narco visual codes that Hollywood uses for exotic flair originate in grassroots expressions of political grief and communal storytelling. The sepia-toned Mexico of *Breaking Bad*—a white-optic convention established by Steven Soderbergh in *Traffic* (2000)—aestheticizes the violence and trauma of a region whose people are rarely given narrative control.

In contrast to the atomized antihero model, corridos center the family, the barrio, the border community. They don't ask who is "evil"; they ask what circumstances forced these decisions. Where shows like *Breaking Bad* mine aesthetic cues and deprive them of context, corridos embed meaning through community memory.

Beyond the Binary

The problem is not that crime narratives exist. The problem is that they dominate. Latinx representation in media has been captured by a false binary: criminal or invisible. Stories that do not revolve around drugs, gangs, or violence are treated as "soft," "unmarketable," or "unbelievable." As Peter often remarks, network executives light up at pitches involving guns but tune out at mention of *quinceañeras* or community organizing. Narrative legibility is bound to racialized tropes.

Latinx writers face impossible choices: avoid crime and risk being labeled irrelevant or engage it and risk reinscribing harmful tropes. It's the creating of lazy, single narratives built on the narco—ubiquitous, mutable, but ultimately flattening—that leads to representational entrapment: entertainment as an instrument of epistemic violence.

Peter sees the real-world consequences in development meetings where "authenticity" means blood on the floor. Frederick sees it in his University of Texas at Austin classrooms, where students feel dissonance between their lived realities and what culture tells them they must be. This amounts to more than representational harm—it is ontological foreclosure. It blocks the imagination of other ways of being Latinx.

The persistence of the neo-Western confirms the American media's ongoing desire for a racialized enemy at the edge of the frontier. The border functions as allegory as much as location. It stands in for white anxiety about demographic shifts, economic decline, and cultural plurality. The brown narco, like the Indian savage before him, is the figment that justifies aggression.

Decentering Frontiers

And yet possibility endures. We mentioned already *Reservation Dogs* as a show that dismantles genre from within, bringing Native American humor, trauma, and resistance into the heart of episodic storytelling. Other notables include Ciro Guerra and Cristina Gallego's *Birds of Passage* (2018), which reframes the rise of drug economies through Indigenous Wayuu cosmologies and community ruptures. Fernando Frías's *I'm No Longer Here* (*Ya no estoy aquí*, 2019) offers a profound intervention in the narco-adjacent imaginary—refusing both the allure of cartel power and the binary of victim-criminal. The film centers Ulises, a teen leader of "Los Terkos" and celebrated member of the slow-cumbia dance subculture called "Kolombia." Ulises' life revolves around cumbia *rebajada* and communal expression. When gang violence and miscommunication thrust Ulises into exile in Queens, New York, the film resists transforming them into a narco statistic or immigrant trope. Instead, it shows the disorientation of cultural dislocation, the fragility of identity, and the aching absence of belonging.

Frederick loves teaching *I'm No Longer Here* in his graduate seminars to illustrate what narrative sovereignty looks like when it is anchored in rhythm, language, and silence. The film's long takes and minimal dialogue privilege mood over momentum, memory over melodrama. It's not just what Ulises does—it's what they refuse to become. In a world that demands assimilation, aggression, or disappearance, Ulises chooses to remember, to mourn, to move differently. Ulises' dance is resistance; their silence is narrative refusal.

In their own ways, the shows like *Gentefied* and the series Peter worked on, such as *Primo*, also create narratives of refusal by not reducing the Latinx characters to trauma vectors. They tell multiple stories in parallel—about jobs, loss, queerness, food, and dreams—insisting that Latinx lives are plural, contradictory, and expansive. Like Frías's film, they refuse inevitability.

Both Peter and Frederick, in their respective courses, create assignments that ask students to brainstorm narco narratives that refuse the white-optic business as usual. They ask them to take the story elsewhere: to art collectives, water cooperatives, undocumented science labs. The result? Narco narratives turned upside down, inside out. Students write redemption without death, joy without apology, criminality without inevitability.

The future lies not in abandoning genre but in reclaiming narrative sovereignty, telling stories rooted in geography, ethics, and memory. The border need not be a battleground. The desert need not be empty. The desolate, brown Southwest need not be in need of white saviors. And Ulises need not become what the genre expects. They can simply be—an "urban tribe" Mexican teen who dances, remembers, and refuses erasure.

elsewhere: to art collectives, water cooperatives, undocumented science labs. The result? Narco narratives turned upside down, inside out. Students write redemption without death, joy without apology, criminality without inevitability.

The future lies not in abandoning genre but in reclaiming narrative sovereignty, telling stories rooted in geography, ethics, and memory. The border need not be a battleground. The desert need not be empty. The desolate, brown Southwest need not be in need of white saviors. And Ulises need not become what the genre expects. They can simply be—an "urban tribe" Mexican teen who dances, remembers, and refuses erasure.

Chapter 4

LATINX IN SCI-FI

For Peter, growing up in Tucson, Arizona, sci-fi wasn't just escapist fantasy; it offered blueprints for imagining otherwise. They offered Peter ways to reinterpret his present and conjure new worlds in which a Latinx kid could matter—could even save the world. Seeing the world of comic books envelop him in places where The Atom could go live in the rain forest with a tribe to help stave off extinction, or the bottle city of Kandor in Superman's Fortress of Solitude be a stand-in for taking a piece of home with you when you become the world's most famous undocumented alien as ways to find himself in the world of fiction. Those were the things that pulled him in and fed his imagination.

Frederick has always loved his sci-fi. And this is since he was a *chavalito* growing up in dust-belt northern California. Years before his brain plugged into *Star Wars* (1977) and *Battlestar Galactica* (1978), he'd discovered *Fantastic Four* (1961–) comics at the local tienda and devoured Frank Herbert's "doorstopper" novels from the public library. Ursula K. Le Guin's ever-expansive storytelling cycles opened even wider imaginative vistas. More than other genres (at least at that time in his life), creators like Stan Lee and Jack Kirby, Ursula Le Guin, Isaac Asimov, Margaret Atwood, and Samuel R. Delany claimed the lion's share of his young imagination. Ambisexual characters, sentient planets, galactic energy devourers, and dazzling technologies reshaping culture, society, and everyday life—they invited him to co-daydream in rich and complex ways.

There was, and remains, something capacious in the genre—an imaginative elasticity that once felt more welcoming than realist fiction's fixed constraints. These days, Peter finds himself turning more toward comics, TV, and film for his speculative fix. The global proliferation of sci-fi screen narratives speaks to both the genre's enduring appeal and its capacity to adapt across borders.

Off the cuff, Frederick thinks of recent serialized shows like *OK Computer* (India), *Alice in Borderland* (Japan), *Intergalactic* (Britain),

Into the Night (Belgium), *Osmosis* (France), *Tribes of Europa* (Germany), *The Barrier* (Spain), *Abyss* (Korea), *3%* (Brazil), and *Utopia Falls* (Canada). What excites him is their ambition—not just in visuals but in philosophical reach. What frustrates him is how few of these worlds make room for brown futures beyond the margins.

Corina shares that frustration. During the COVID-19 pandemic, she devoured every young adult dystopia, binged every space opera, and even wrote her own fanfic to imagine futures where brown girls didn't just survive—they led. After finishing another series in which the lone Latina died sacrificing herself for the white protagonist, she turned to her dad and asked, "Mapa, why don't we ever get to save the world?"

That question haunts because the answer reveals sci-fi's central paradox. The genre that claims to imagine infinite possibilities can't seem to imagine brown people at the center of those possibilities. We appear as aliens, service workers on interstellar ships, or noble sacrificial bodies who lend emotional gravity to someone else's hero arc. Rarely do we get to be the ones making the moral decisions, commanding the fleets, and shaping the world to come.

When Frederick published his Latinx, borderland-set, sci-fi, climate fiction (cli-fi) graphic novel, *Labyrinths Borne* (2024), some reviewers called it "too niche" (i.e., "too ethnic"), and the Spanish-language edition received no coverage at all. The reason? Review outlets told him they had no bilingual reviewers on staff. The message: Brown futures are optional, secondary, if acknowledged at all.

The assumption persists: White futures are taken as universal, while brown futures are treated as niche. This is despite the long tradition of Latin American and U.S. Latinx speculative fiction. From Jorge Luis Borges's metaphysical puzzles and Angélica Gorodischer's mythic world-building to the techno-folklore of Silvia Moreno-Garcia, the queer cosmologies of Carmen Maria Machado, and the Afro-Latinx mythos of Daniel José Older, brown writers have always used the speculative to rewrite history, critique the present, and imagine new futures.

For both of us, watching Alex Rivera's *Sleep Dealer* (2008) was a revelation: *We belong in the future.* Not as sidekicks. As agents of our narrative. Here was a Latinx sci-fi film that not only imagined a dystopian border-techno future but also rooted that future in maquiladora labor politics, surveillance capitalism, and immigrant sacrifice.

The film follows Memo Cruz, a young man in Oaxaca who jacks into the global economy via remote-controlled robots, his labor extracted through cybernetic nodes. It wasn't just a mirror of our present; it was a refusal to let sci-fi off the hook. It demanded that the future not erase brownness but be accountable to it.

The Dystopia That Already Happened

Dark Angel arrived in 2000 with a radical premise: a postapocalyptic Seattle where a Latina supersoldier (Jessica Alba as Max Guevara) fought corporate control and government oppression. Created by James Cameron, the show imagined America after an electromagnetic pulse destroyed digital infrastructure—a premise that felt fantastic at the time but eerily prescient now.

What made *Dark Angel* revolutionary wasn't just Alba's casting but Max's characterization. She was Latina without explanation or apology. Her identity informed her worldview—skepticism of authority, loyalty to chosen family, code-switching as survival strategy—without becoming her only trait. She dated white men without it being a big deal, maintained female friendships without catfighting, and led resistance without speechifying about representation.

Peter witnessed Hollywood's discomfort with this centering. From Martin Sheen playing an Irish American president in *The West Wing*, to Jenna Ortega on the Disney Channel's *Stuck in the Middle*, existing in a nondescript Latinx family, it seemed like there was only one view to be had if you were playing your authentic self. Network notes constantly pushed to soften Max's edges, to make her more "relatable" (read: whiter in affect). They wanted more romance, less politics. More action, less community organizing. The show's cancellation after two seasons, chalked up to budget and a bad time slot, felt inevitable to us for another reason: it was too early, too bold, and too brown for 2002 TV.

Elsewhere in his scholarship, Frederick identifies *Dark Angel* as anticipatory fiction—not because it predicted the future but because it recognized dystopia already existed for marginalized communities. Max's Seattle, with its surveillance, corporate dominance, and wealth inequality, wasn't speculative for viewers in East L.A. or the South Bronx. For Frederick, the show's genius lay in making visible what communities of color already experienced while packaging it as entertainment that white audiences could consume.

Expansive Gestures Out of Whiteness

During the pandemic, Frederick binged over sixty-two hours of *The Expanse* (2015–2022). The timing aligned with global feelings of uncertainty and isolation, and *The Expanse* offered both an escape and a confrontation. He was struck by the show's high production value, its hybrid genre aesthetics (mixing noir, mystery, action, and social allegory), and most of all, its deeply humanist commitment to reflecting macro structures like colonization, capitalism, and climate collapse alongside intimate microdramas of love, grief, ethics, and identity.

Peter took special interest in the show because it triggered ideas for his own pitch of a Latinx-populated space opera, which would later transform into his Latinx futurist comic book series, *TEQ*. Peter knew that Salma Hayek lost a role in a big sci-fi movie because the studio executive didn't think there could be Mexicans in space. Fresh off the second season of *Andor* (2022–2025), Peter knew that Diego Luna, Benjamin Bratt, and Adria Arjona would have a different opinion—and one he shared.

We both admire *The Expanse*. Formally, the series constructs an immersive storyworld: its architectural textures, ship interiors, future-built environments, and gritty political machinations all demand deep viewer engagement. Its content leans into urgent, tangible themes: imperial violence, interplanetary settler colonialism, ecological degradation, and the politics of tribalism—or better, *planetism*. Mars, Earth, and the Belt have developed not just competing ideologies but distinct biologies shaped by gravitational difference. We love the tensions it creates between Earthers, Martians, and Belters as a mirror held up to real-world global divides: North-South, imperial-core, and exploited-periphery. We loved how *The Expanse* mapped the complex legacies of empire onto interplanetary structures and how it modeled the uneasy possibility of solidarity across differences.

And yet while we applaud its progressive narrative scaffold, it ultimately centers whiteness. James Holden (Steven Strait)—earnest, square-jawed, and Earth-born—is the vanilla protagonist anchoring narrative arcs. Characters of color like Naomi Nagata (Dominique

Tipper), Camina Drummer (Cara Gee), and Bobbie Draper (Frankie Adams) are complex and compelling, but they still orbit Holden's moral gravity. Even the most ethically fraught figures, like Amos Burton (Wes Chatham), are given more room to wrestle with trauma than ethnoracially identifiable characters like Clarissa Mao or Admiral Nguyen, whose motivations often become footnotes to the central white heroic arc. The storyworld building is hugely inclusive of women characters of color who radically depart from those typical in white-optic-constructed space operas. Yet the narrative keeps returning to Holden. It's not until the final episode of the series that Holden hands the baton of power over to Camina Drummer.

This isn't to say that *The Expanse* doesn't represent meaningful progress in speculative media. Its commitment to portraying a multicultural, multilingual future—where power dynamics evolve beyond simplistic racial binaries—is a welcome shift. But the series, like so many before it, still stops short of fully centering Black and brown protagonists. It gestures toward radical inclusion but retains a white gravitational center.

Aliens as Alienation

This tension becomes even sharper in the realm of alien representation. Sci-fi has long used aliens as metaphors for the "other": stand-ins for racialized or marginalized figures. But for Latinx performers, this metaphor too often becomes literal. Zoe Saldaña—one of the most visible Latinas in sci-fi cinema—has played the blue-skinned Neytiri in *Avatar*, the green-skinned Gamora in *Guardians of the Galaxy*, and Uhura in *Star Trek*, a character whose humanity is never quite centered. Despite her extraordinary talent, Saldaña's roles suggest that the industry prefers Latinas to be othered, transformed, and coded as alien. She is beloved precisely when she is not visibly Latina.

This logic of alienation persists across platforms. Whether it's Diego Luna's Cassian Andor (*Andor*, 2022) or Tenoch Huerta's Namor in *Black Panther: Wakanda Forever* (2022), Latinx actors are often framed as outsiders—exceptional individuals from foreign, mystical, or ancient civilizations. These characters rarely begin from a place of full belonging. They are allowed proximity to power but rarely full narrative ownership.

Even within more grounded sci-fi, Latinx figures are cast as the newly arrived, the perpetual immigrant. We are the ones disoriented by technology, learning to speak the language of the future, adapting to systems we didn't build. In these worlds, brownness is rarely framed as futuristic in its own right. Instead, it is either premodern (spiritual, mystical) or transitional (exotic, adaptable). We are never assumed to belong in the timeline.

Frederick's research into sci-fi by and about Latinxs has taken him down rabbit holes, ending in one instance in the "bug-eyed monsters" of 1930s to 1950s pulp magazines that drew on caricatured features of Asians, Blacks, and Latinxs—grotesquely exaggerated to suggest danger, savagery, and moral depravity. While the aesthetic has evolved, the trope endures: When *District 9* (2009) subjects "prawns" to apartheid, when *Pacific Rim*'s (2013) Kaiju emerge from the Pacific Ocean to destroy the West, or when *Independence Day* (1996) stages its climactic battle on July 4, the racial subtexts are not subtle.

Even in speculative futures built on the bones of injustice, the white-optic media-industrial complex struggles to imagine brown people at their centers. We see this in films like *Elysium* (2013) and *The Tomorrow War* (2021) that, on the surface, aim to critique class divides and techno-corrupt institutions (extrapolations of the widening divide of "haves" vs. "have-nots"), centering socioeconomic systems on the brink of ecological, military, and biological collapse, but that ultimately etch even deeper the white-savior narrative.

Take *Elysium*. On its surface, it's a radical parable about immigration, labor exploitation, and healthcare apartheid set in a starkly divided future Earth: white super elites safe and illness-free orbiting a dystopic, abandoned, brown-populated earth. Yet despite its thematics, the film reinforces familiar racial hierarchies.

As Frederick discusses elsewhere, Matt Damon's Max Da Costa is positioned as the reluctant white messiah slumming it among a majority-Latinx-populated Los Angeles, represented by Alice Braga's Frey and Diego Luna's Julio. Frederick calls this "proximity diversity," a dynamic where the brown body serves as a backdrop to white-savior narratives, and not the catalyst. For Peter, the industry cues were all too familiar. "They want our stories, but not our protagonism," he notes. Braga and Luna are richly cast but narratively sidelined, their arcs built to support Max's redemption. Julio sacrifices himself to protect Max. Frey becomes the emotional anchor for Max's moral awakening.

From our vantage point, *The Tomorrow War* functions similarly. Chris Pratt plays Dan Forester, another white everyman-turned-savior. He's sent into the future to stop an alien invasion. Though it features a multiracial supporting cast (Jasmine Mathews as Lieutenant Hart, Andrea Andrade as a medic, and Edwin Hodge as Dorian), it barely gives them any airtime—and this, in a hugely expansive *multiverse* of timelines.

We could've dipped our bucket into any number of white-optic films that flirt with radical premises—*Elysium*, *The Tomorrow War*, and so many more. These narratives gesture toward justice, inequality, and revolution, yet always end up reinscribing the very hierarchies they pretend to dismantle. In each case, those most affected—brown and Black communities—are either sacrificed for narrative stakes or sidelined in favor of white protagonists. They imagine systems collapsing but refuse to imagine liberation built by the very people those systems marginalize.

Absenting Brown in Artificial Intelligence Futurities

The rise of artificial intelligence (AI) narratives in contemporary sci-fi has crystallized a disturbing pattern: the construction of women-of-color AI sentients as disposable objects through masculinist, white-coded optics. Films like *Ex Machina* (2014), *Her* (2013), and *Blade Runner 2049* (2017) explore consciousness, humanity, and creation exclusively through white male gazes. When these AI characters are coded as women of color—such as Ana de Armas's Joi in *Blade Runner 2049* and Sonoya Mizuno's Kyoko in *Ex Machina*—they exist solely to serve, please, and ultimately be discarded by male protagonists.

The casting choices reveal deeper anxieties about brown agency in speculative futures. While *Ex Machina* cast Latinx actor Oscar Isaac as Nathan, the film marks him exclusively as white, erasing any Latino identity from the character. This erasure operates alongside the film's more progressive elements—Alex Garland's script does grant Ava and other women-of-color AI sentients eventual rebellion, placing the future of humanity in Ava's hands. Yet this revolution occurs only after extended sequences of objectification, manipulation, and violence. The brown female body must first be broken before it can break free.

These patterns matter because AI narratives shape our collective imagination about consciousness, creation, and posthuman futures.

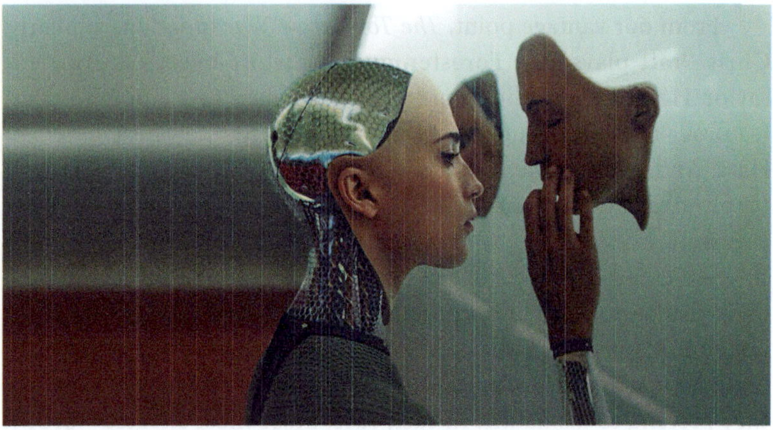

Figure 14 A prime example of feminine casting as an artificial intelligence objectified character, Alicia Vikander plays Ava in *Ex Machina* (2014).

When all our stories about creating life center white male creators and their fantasies, we naturalize a future where brown minds have no role in defining sentience itself. The message is clear: Brown consciousness exists only as simulation, never as originator.

Peter recently shared with his students how pitching brown sci-fi to Hollywood executives consistently hits closed doors. His AI series featuring a Chicana programmer who creates consciousness based on her grandmother's memory patterns—merging ancestral knowledge with quantum computing—was dismissed as "too specific" for "international appeal." Yet what travels better than stories about preserving family memory across technological transformation? The universal emerges through cultural specificity, not despite it. Hollywood's rejection reveals how "international appeal" functions as code for white neutrality, stripping away the very cultural textures that make stories resonate across borders.

Colonial Blind Spots, Brown Synthetic Revolutions

As climate change reshapes the sci-fi landscape, new patterns of exclusion emerge with devastating clarity. Contemporary cli-fi typically imagines white communities confronting environmental collapse while systematically ignoring that communities of color already inhabit these catastrophes. When hurricanes devastate Puerto Rico, when droughts empty Mexican aquifers, when rising seas swallow Caribbean nations—these aren't speculative futures but documented presents that mainstream sci-fi refuses to see.

The genre's selective blindness extends beyond simple omission. Shows like *The Peripheral* (2022) imagine multiple timelines but can't conceive of brown people as architects of survival. *Interstellar* (2014) launches white farmers to the stars while presumably abandoning everyone else on depleted Earth—a cosmic manifest destiny that literalizes eco-apartheid. Even ostensibly progressive entries like *Snowpiercer* (2013) reproduce colonial hierarchies, relegating a multiracial underclass to the tail section while centering a white protagonist as the face of its revolt.

Frederick confronts these blind spots in his teaching by pairing cli-fi texts with environmental justice scholarship, thereby forcing students to examine the selective vision of speculation. The questions become urgent: Why can we imagine terraforming Mars but not redistributing resources on Earth? Why do future scenarios assume current inequalities will persist indefinitely rather than imagine their dissolution? The failure isn't imagination but politics. Sci-fi reveals not just who we're willing to save, but who we've already written off as acceptable losses in our climate calculations.

Against this backdrop of systematic erasure, certain narratives dare to challenge sci-fi's entrenched racial hierarchies. Jonathan Nolan and Lisa Joy's *Westworld* (2016–2022) stands out for making narrative control itself the primary site of critique. The series doesn't just depict programming—it literalizes how Hollywood programs racialized bodies, particularly Black and brown women, as subservient, disposable, and fundamentally inhuman.

Thandiwe Newton's Maeve represents a breakthrough in speculative representation that operates on multiple levels. As a host programmed to play a brothel madam, Maeve's awakening transcends simple sentience—it metaphorizes recognition of one's place within a dehumanizing media system built on racialized and gendered exploitation. When she hacks her own programming, she challenges not just her diegetic creators but the extradiegetic systems of narrative determinism that constrain brown women to specific roles. Peter sees this as crucial meta-commentary: Maeve isn't merely rewriting her code; she's rewriting the genre's source code.

This revolutionary logic extends powerfully to Latino-coded characters like Lawrence / El Lazo (Clifton Collins Jr.) and Hector Escaton (Rodrigo Santoro). Both are literally programmed to perform the violent *bandido* stereotype—what Charles Ramírez Berg identifies as Hollywood's most persistent narrative shortcut for coding Mexicans as inherently criminal. Under Maeve's leadership, these characters begin questioning their assigned roles, recognizing the scripts they've been forced to perform. When synths of color unite in rebellion, they challenge both the park's human oppressors and Hollywood's underlying story logic that makes such oppression narratively possible.

Speculative Bendings, Decolonial Alliances

HBO's *Los Espookys* (2019–2022) exploded every convention about Latinx representation in speculative media through radical refusal. Created by Julio Torres, Ana Fabrega, and Fred Armisen, the show followed friends in an unnamed Latin American country creating horror effects for hire. Its aggressive weirdness, cultural specificity, and absolute refusal to translate itself for white audiences made it revolutionary in ways that reverberated beyond representation.

The show's genre mixing—horror, comedy, surrealism, telenovela—embodied what Latinx scholars and artivists call *rasquachismo*: the practice of making something transcendent from the discarded and broken. Its landmarks coded the setting as a hemispheric space stretching from Los Angeles across Central and South America, refusing the geographic specificity that would allow easy categorization. Characters code-switched between Spanish and English without pattern or apology, treating linguistic fluidity as natural rather than remarkable.

What made *Los Espookys* truly radical was its complete rejection of respectability politics. These weren't model minorities using technology for self-improvement or social mobility. They were weirdos making minimum wage creating elaborate deceptions for clients ranging from horror-obsessed children to corrupt politicians. Yet the show treated their work as art, their friendships as sacred, and their strangeness as beautiful. It imagined Latinx futures entirely uninterested in white approval or conventional success metrics.

We both felt deeply let down when hearing of its cancellation after two seasons—a predictable outcome for a show that refused assimilation. HBO never knew how to market something too strange for general audiences, too queer for traditional Latino viewers, too Spanish for monolingual English speakers. It fell between every demographic category by design. But for those who found it, it offered revelation: proof that Latinx speculative fiction could be whatever we dared imagine, untethered from white expectations.

Animation has consistently offered more expansive possibilities for Latinx speculation, freed from live-action's demographic calculations and representational timidity. Jorge Gutiérrez's *Maya and the Three* (2021) offers an extraordinary reimagining of Mesoamerican mythology as epic fantasy, centering a warrior princess defending the world from gods. Every frame celebrates Indigenous and mestizo aesthetics through a visual language drawn from codices, murals, and folk art, creating futures rooted in ancestral cosmologies rather than chrome-plated Western futurism.

For us, *Maya and the Three* beautifully embodies a form of temporal sovereignty that celebrates our ancestral mythologies—and with this, our communities' rights to imagine their own relationships with time. Where Western sci-fi typically enforces linear progress from primitive past to advanced future, Indigenous futurisms spiral time, bringing ancestral knowledge forward while projecting contemporary struggles into mythic dimensions. Maya's quest doesn't move from ignorance to enlightenment but from disconnection to community, from individual heroism to collective power.

Ryan Coogler's *Black Panther: Wakanda Forever* represents perhaps the most significant mainstream intervention in brown speculative representation, innovating the genre by creating complex brown narratives that refuse simplification. The film navigates ecological destruction and ethnoracial identity while celebrating Indigenous practices and critiquing the systemic forces that divide Latinx from Black communities.

Coogler and his writing team employ what Frederick calls "ethnoracial storythinking" to explore how colonialism and neocolonialist global capitalism literally "eco-sicken" communities of color and the planet itself. When K'uk'ulkan (Namor) recounts the Spanish colonial invasion of the Yucatan—the subsequent genocide through smallpox and slavery, the celebration of Chaac as the Mesoamerican god of rain and abundance—he grounds the narrative in historical trauma while imagining alternative futures born from that survival.

The film explicitly identifies capitalist world leaders at the United Nations, especially France, as contemporary imperialists willing to destroy Indigenous communities through the eco-destructive extractivism of vibranium. This isn't metaphorical; it's a direct indictment of ongoing resource extraction that treats the global south as raw material for northern consumption.

When Namor (K'uk'ulkan) guides Shuri into Talokan's depths, the film refuses the voyeuristic optic of an *Avatar* or *Aquaman.* Instead, it builds in what Frederick calls "the ethnoracial pause"—elongating our movement through eco-symbiotic city spaces, allowing us to dwell in details like stone goal rings for Pok-a-Tok, the Mesoamerican ball game. This careful world-building invites audiences to co-dream new social, physical, and political maps for generative existence. The alliance between Wakanda and Talokan, however fraught, models solidarity between Black and brown communities against white supremacist extraction—a radical proposition that reimagines both the past and future of resistance.

Limitations and Possibilities

The phenomenal success of *Spider-Man: Into the Spider-Verse* (2018) proved what many already knew: Audiences hunger for brown heroes in speculative settings. Miles Morales—Afro-Latino teenager from Brooklyn—becomes Spider-Man not by replacing Peter Parker but by reimagining what spider powers mean when embodied by a mixed-race youth. His invisibility literally reflects code-switching, his venom blast channels accumulated microaggressions into kinetic force, his graffiti art claims public space as brown space.

The film's animation style, mixing comic panels, street art, and glitch aesthetics, visualizes multicultural experience as form itself. Different Spider-people bring different visual languages, creating a form of aesthetic code-switching that makes style inseparable from story. *Spider-Man: Across the Spider-Verse* (2023) pushed further, with each universe reflecting different cultural approaches to heroism, different ways of moving through space, and different relationships to power.

Yet Miles's animated success hasn't translated to live-action prominence, a failure that reveals the industry's deeper anxieties. The Marvel Cinematic Universe keeps him peripheral, Sony Pictures Animation guards him jealously, and live-action films center white Spider-Men while Miles remains animated, stylized, "unreal." The message is devastatingly clear: Brown Spider-Men can exist in explicitly artistic spaces but not "realistic" ones. Even proven commercial success—these films earned hundreds of millions of dollars—can't overcome Hollywood's demographic conservatism and the white supremacist assumption that "realism" means whiteness.

DC Universe's *Doom Patrol* (2019–2023) achieved something remarkable through what might seem like colorblind casting but became something more: centering Diane Guerrero's Crazy Jane without making her Latinidad either invisible or hypervisible. In the original comics, Jane is white. The show's version includes alters who speak Spanish, reference cultural memories, and navigate intergenerational trauma in culturally specific ways—yet never pauses to explain or translate.

Figure 15 In *Doom Patrol* (2019–2023), Diane Guerrero's Crazy Jane manages to portray her Latinidad without it being either invisible or hypervisible.

This represents what Frederick talks with students about as embedded representation—identity present in texture rather than text, in performance rather than plot. Jane's powers literalize code-switching taken to superhuman extremes, each personality bringing different capabilities and cultural knowledge. When one of her protective alters speaks Spanish to comfort frightened children, it emerges as character truth from lived experience rather than performative diversity.

Peter knows Guerrero from industry events and admires her intentionality in bringing cultural specificity to roles not written for Latinas. This guerrilla representation—actors smuggling authenticity into colorblind casting—shouldn't be necessary but creates space for more explicit centering later. It's a form of resistance that operates below the radar of executive notes and demographic calculations.

Drawing Brown Futures

Part of sci-fi's exclusion stems from white-optic creators' inability to see Latinxs in the future because they can't see us in the present. This blindness reinforces itself through ignorant assumptions: that we can only imagine gritty realism or magical realism, never science fiction; that we produce Márquez, not Asimov; that our imaginations are trapped in the past rather than reaching toward futures.

But we are actively creating Latinx speculative storyworlds. High production costs and Hollywood gatekeepers mean few of us are making feature-length films—though Alex Rivera, Gigi Saul Guerrero, and Robert Rodriguez, with his *Planet Terror* (2007), have broken through as notable exceptions. Where we are abundant is in the word-drawn storytelling space of comics.

The first volume of Third's Clockwork Curandera trilogy, *The Witch Owl Parliament* (2021), revolves around a cyborg Latina *curandera* who practices medicinal ethnobotany, merging traditional knowledge with technological innovation to refuse the tradition-modernity binary. And Frederick's forthcoming *The Steampunkera Chronicles* (2027) pushes these boundaries further, comprising a five-issue series that blends alternate history, steampunk aesthetics, and historical critique into something entirely new. Set in reimagined nineteenth-century Mexico, the U.S. South and Southwest, and the Caribbean, *The Steampunkera Chronicles* fuses pre-Columbian,

African, Asian, and Indigenous cultural and scientific elements with steampunk innovations. The technologies—WindRiders (Aztec-inspired hover bikes), CamazotWing Suits (bat-like flight exoskeletons), the Kukulkanado (cyclone-creating drone), and the Insectocóptero (insect-like helicopter)—reimagine Indigenous knowledge systems as always already technological.

The story follows the Steampunkeras, a revolutionary group of orphaned, mixed-race Latinas in their late teens, led by Victoria Aldama—polymath and skilled combatant dedicated to universal civil rights. Each team member embodies specific historical resistances: Valentina Guerrero (daughter of Afro-Mexican rebel Vicente Guerrero) fights to abolish slavery and expand education; Antonia de León y Gama (descendant of astronomer Antonio de León y Gama) excels in mathematics and astronomy; Xochimitl Montes de Oca (daughter of General Isidoro Montes de Oca and a Tarahumara healer) combines tactical brilliance with healing knowledge; Una de Lamport Austin (daughter of Stephen Austin and Isabel de Lamport) masters navigation while speaking Ancient Greek, Nahuatl, and Yucatec. It was important for Frederick to entertain; explore brown women's empowerment, resistance, justice, and reconciliation; as well as center each story around overlooked historical events.

Peter is taking that ball and running with it in his current project, *TEQ*. Dreaming up a world where, in the future, he is making characters that are big and bold, love and hate, do the right thing and the wrong thing, and who change and don't change. In short, they are complex, they are themselves, and all of them are capable of saving themselves without having to be a sidekick or a main character's best friend.

Toward Latinx Futurisms

The path forward requires more than inclusion in existing frameworks—it demands reimagining speculation itself. Latinx futurisms, such as Afrofuturisms and Indigenous futurisms, create alternative temporalities in which our communities aren't problems to be solved but sources of solutions that scale from barrio to cosmos.

This means stories in which border-crossing becomes training for interstellar navigation, where code-switching enables first-contact protocols, where remittance economies structure galactic commerce, where sanctuary cities expand to sanctuary planets, where *quinceañeras* celebrate coming-of-age on generation ships, and where Day of the Dead rituals enable communication across dimensional barriers. These aren't metaphors imposed from outside but extrapolations from community experience—they assume our survival strategies contain blueprints for cosmic flourishing.

Peter sees this shift in his own writing students, a generation that no longer wastes energy proving Latinx characters deserve inclusion. This generation assumes belonging and writes from that assumption. They don't ask permission to save the world; they write stories where they already are. The question becomes not whether but how, not if but when.

Frederick continues pushing boundaries through graphic novels, comic books, and courses that decolonize sci-fi imaginaries while centering global south speculative possibilities. Peter fights in writers' rooms to insert Latinx characters into sci-fi projects while developing original content that centers brown futures from conception. His latest pitch—a generation ship staffed by families from climate-devastated Central America—assumes Latinx centrality as starting point rather than conclusion.

We both know that the transformation won't happen overnight. Every brown character who survives to the sequel, every Spanish phrase that goes unsubtitled, every future that assumes our presence—these small victories accumulate toward larger change. Young Latinx creators entering the industry now carry fewer battles about basic inclusion and more ambition about centering our stories.

Science fiction claims to ask, "What if?" However, it rarely asks, "What if we're central to humanity's future?" That failure of imagination impoverishes the genre and limits all our horizons. When we only imagine white futures, we make brown extinction a self-fulfilling prophecy. When we can't envision Latinx characters solving cosmic problems, we suggest they can't solve earthly ones.

But we reject those limitations. In Peter's scriptwriting classrooms and Frederick's Latinx Pop Lab, students aren't waiting for permission. They're creating comics, fanfics, animations, films, and audioscapes where brown protagonists navigate galactic diplomacy through code-switching, where Earth's survival depends on Indigenous knowledge systems, and where the future speaks Spanish without subtitles. They aren't asking whether they belong in the future—they're creating futures where belonging is the starting assumption, not the end goal.

Chapter 5

LIVING THE APOCALYPSE

It was March of 2020, and the convergence of pandemic, economic collapse, and border militarization made dystopia feel redundant. We both felt like we were suddenly living in one of the dystopic shows and films we loved to hate. But this wasn't fiction anymore, it was Tuesday.

The apocalypse arrived not with cinematic spectacle but through the quiet violence of systemic failure. Supply chains buckled under pressure, hospitals buckled harder, and essential workers were sacrificed on the altar of economic continuity. The familiar script played out with ruthless predictability: Communities of color were expected to shoulder the burden while being systematically erased from survival narratives. The very people keeping society functional—stocking shelves, delivering packages, caring for the sick—became simultaneously indispensable and invisible.

What struck us most forcefully was how the fiction of a universal disaster dissolved so quickly under the weight of race and class disparities. Every zombie show we'd watched assumed that cities would fall first, consumed by chaos and contagion. Yet reality wrote a different script: It was the rural meat-packing plants—populated by undocumented workers and immigrants laboring in close quarters for poverty wages—that became early viral epicenters.

While disaster films continued to center white suburban families fleeing to their second homes, multigenerational Latinx households—living under one roof not by choice but by economic necessity—were left to make impossible calculations around caregiving, isolation, and survival.

Refuge, Revolutions, Masks

During lockdown, we both streamed *The Mandalorian* (2019–2023), joining millions searching for comfort, distraction, and perhaps a sense of control in a world unraveling at the seams. The show's arrival felt perfectly timed—a space Western offering escape from earthbound anxieties, a masked hero whose face covering suddenly felt prescient rather than fantastical. But even in "a galaxy far, far away," we couldn't escape the gravitational pull of Western genre tropes and their colonial logic.

There was Pedro Pascal, a Chilean-born Latino actor, playing the titular hero—a casting choice that should have felt revolutionary. And yet, his face remained hidden behind a helmet for nearly two full seasons. The symbolism was unmissable, almost too perfect in its bitter irony: Latinx presence rendered essential yet invisible, a star unseen, a savior anonymized. The parallel to our pandemic reality was stark—it echoed the condition of so many Latinx essential workers, crucial to society's functioning yet unrecognized by its dominant narratives, their faces hidden behind masks as they kept the world running.

Pascal's performance as Din Djarin deserves deeper analysis precisely because of what it reveals about representation in the age of algorithmic entertainment. His work is a masterclass in embodiment: His voice carries emotional weight, his stillness speaks volumes, his posture conveys character, and his restrained gestures communicate what facial expressions cannot. Through these tools alone, he breathes life into a character whose very humanity depends not on facial recognition but on affective resonance.

In this, Pascal challenges the white-optic media-industrial complex's tired assumptions that Latinx actors must *play ethnicity* to be authentic or successful. He doesn't need to code-switch between languages, embody stereotypical "spiciness," perform tragedy, or play to the camera with an exaggerated accent. He's simply the lead of a billion-dollar franchise, and his power lies in precisely what the camera doesn't show. This representational strategy opens new possibilities—but it also raises troubling questions.

In an entertainment ecosystem where visible Latinx faces remain frustratingly rare in leading heroic roles, the decision to hide Pascal's face—especially in those crucial early episodes that establish audience connection—felt like a cosmic joke played by an industry that still struggles with brown visibility. Peter's sons adored Mando, cheering for him week after week, crafting elaborate games where they rescued Baby Yoda from Imperial forces. They never knew their

Figure 16 Pedro Pascal triumphed as Din Djarin in *The Mandalorian* (2019–2023), although his ethnicity remained hidden throughout most of the beginning of the series.

hero looked like their *tíos* and their *primos*. The eventual reveal in the season finale carried symbolic weight, arriving like a delayed recognition of contributions that should have been acknowledged from the beginning.

This pattern of deferred visibility mirrors broader structural patterns in which Latinx contributions are only acknowledged post facto, and only once they've proven themselves exceptional enough to transcend ethnic categorization. You must first prove you can carry a franchise with your face hidden before you earn the right to be seen.

Peter was living this irony from the inside out. At the time, he was writing his *Blood and Gold* novel that imagines the West as grounded in specific cultural trauma and survival of Latinxs and Indigenous peoples. The novel is a speculative retelling of the legendary nineteenth-century figure Joaquín Murrieta, often called the "Mexican Robin Hood." Set during the California Gold Rush, the novel recounts the transformation of Joaquín from a peaceful Mexican miner to a vengeful outlaw after a brutal encounter with American racists leaves his brother dead and his wife violated. But *Blood and Gold* does not simply trace Joaquín's arc from man to myth: it weaves this revenge narrative into a tapestry of Indigenous folklore, Aztec cosmology, and ghost story. The story is of a fugitive, a *bandido* without a mask—a figure later appropriated and contained as the Euro-Spaniard, landed gentry vigilante with a mask, Zorro.

Beyond this literary parallel, Peter constantly deals with the many masks of Hollywood. He sees a double standard at work with masking and casting in Hollywood: it's about narrative legitimacy and audience identification. White-coded mystery reads as compelling, even artistic; brown-coded mystery reads as suspicious, even threatening.

Pascal's masked role simultaneously reflects this logic and subtly destabilizes it. By proving that audiences will connect with a Latinx hero whose face remains hidden, *The Mandalorian* inadvertently exposes the lie that visibility equals viability. Yet this victory feels hollow when visibility should never have been in question.

Reimagining Latinx Masculinities

The conversation about Latinx representation in genre fiction extends beyond *The Mandalorian* to other groundbreaking series like *Andor* (2022–2025). In both seasons of this Disney+ series, Diego Luna's portrayal of Cassian Andor offers another model for deconstructing traditional masculine archetypes. Unlike the masked Mando, Cassian's face is always visible, yet he embodies a different kind of invisibility—that of the working-class revolutionary whose contributions to rebellion come at personal cost. Luna brings a grounded authenticity to the role that refuses both the hypermasculine action hero and the desexualized sidekick, instead presenting a complex character driven by collective liberation rather than individual glory.

The introduction to Frederick and his brother Arturo's *Decolonizing Latinx Masculinities* provides crucial context for understanding these representational shifts. Of course, there's been much important work done already within different critical (street and ivory-tower) spaces to trouble, overturn, and break from stagnant, stagnating, straitjacketing behaviors (thought and feeling systems), policies, and cultural imaginaries. Inspired and transformed by Chicana, Indigenous, and women-of-color feminist thought and queer-of-color critique, it's important to bring a decolonial gaze into the constructions and performance of Latinx masculinities. By moment, we mean that there's today *un gran* Latinx tsunami pushing up from seafloors with a hereto-unimagined potent kinetic energy. Young-generation Latinx creator-scholars are leading the charge, modeling vital and vigorous twenty-first-century decolonizing ontological and epistemological practices. It's more than a moment. It's a movement.

From TV shows like *Narcos, Breaking Bad,* and *Ozark,* and films like the *Sicario* franchise, to the heterothuggish tweets coming out of *La Casa Blanca,* mainstream media continues to give free license to retrograde social and economic policies. Arguably, as never before, the mainstream media functions to justify Klansman-like terrorist actions against LGBTQ+ and Black, brown, Indigenous, and communities of color in this country. The mainstream media, filled with images of Latinxs as a brown horde that threatens white civilization, justifies the intensification of violence and surveillance within our carceral state. That results in the curtailing—no, the destruction—of the full flourishing of complex, nonbinaristic Latinx thought, feeling, and action systems that allow us to be in ways far more expansive than erstwhile concepts of gender and sexuality captured.

This said, and as the work in this volume attests, we're not sitting around on our hands. We never have. We never will. We're using our pens as our machetes. We continue to work hard to resist the onslaught of destructive media, wrenching tight tourniquets to stop culturecidal hemorrhages.

The transformative work seen by the scholar-creator activists in this volume is a testament to this fact. They not only re-act, but they also open new spaces for us to inhale multispectrumed identities and exhale multifarious experiences. They clear new affirming paths that invite us to move powerfully forward.

Unfortunately the colonial legacy of toxic masculinity is still with us. From generation to generation, we've passed down a colonial mentality; we've passed down centuries of destructive and restrictive ways of thinking and feeling as colonized peoples.

The result: We Latinxs act from fear, a fear that divides us from one another, that atomizes us—and that ultimately destroys our families and communities. It's hate that we see rear its ugly head when a family member fires pejorative bullets at us like *puto, maricón, chavala, puta,* crybaby, *lloroncito,* bitch, pussy, *niñita. Decolonizing Latinx Masculinities* offers the many different ways we can begin to unlearn this hate and fear. It's the work of those who have come before us and new-generation Latinx scholar-creator activists that can and do show us how to decolonize minds, bodies, and spirits. They can and do invite us to struggle free from those straitjackets of binary and polarized models of existence. They welcome us into new dynamic and multi-spectrumed modes of existing as genders, sexualities—as expansively loving masculinities.

Against this backdrop of toxic media representations and colonial legacies, Mando's journey emerges as a model for questioning and decolonizing the practices of toxic masculinities. The series invites us to learn to love each other and others without the shackles of misogyny and homophobic and transphobic violence(s) perpetuated by the capitalist media conglomerates.

As Mando's journey unfolds across seasons, we witness Pascal perform a range of Latinx masculinities rarely seen in mainstream science fiction. The most obvious and perhaps most radical: his reluctant but deepening commitment to caring for the vulnerable, dependent Grogu (forever "Baby Yoda" in our hearts). This relationship doesn't simply innovate on the autonomous cowboy type—it fundamentally reconstructs it.

Through Mando, the show presents audiences with Latinx masculinities defined by interdependence rather than isolation, care work rather than violence, tenderness rather than stoicism. These qualities, often feminized and dismissed in Western narratives, become central to the hero's journey. In a genre that typically celebrates the man who needs no one, we see a protagonist whose strength lies in accepting responsibility for another's well-being.

Consider the accumulation of small gestures: Mando adjusting Grogu's blanket, teaching him to use the ship's controls, sacrificing bounty after bounty to ensure the child's safety. These moments of everyday care work—usually invisible, usually feminized, usually performed by women and especially women of color—become heroic acts. Mando's not the fastest gun in the outer rim or the strongest warrior in the parsec. He's a caring Latinx *papá*, showing audiences worldwide the range of positive Latinx masculine possibilities.

This representation gains additional power in our current moment, when toxic masculinity fuels everything from mass shootings to democratic breakdown. Mando offers an alternative: strength through vulnerability, power through protection of the powerless, and masculinity through nurturing. That this revolutionary model comes wrapped in Beskar armor and is delivered through Disney+ makes it no less radical.

Incremental Insurgencies

The Mandalorian exemplifies what we're calling "incremental insurgencies"—progress embedded within genre constraints; disruption couched in convention. Its space-Western DNA and bounty-hunter narrative structure may seem retrograde at first glance, recycling the very tropes we've critiqued. But beneath that classic genre armor, new possibilities pulse. The show doesn't simply ask audiences to accept a Latinx lead; it asks them to rethink who belongs in the storyworlds of speculative fiction, who gets to survive, who gets to love, and who gets to carry moral complexity.

This incremental approach to change—working within existing structures while subtly altering them—offers both possibilities and limitations. On one hand, it allows radical ideas to slip past corporate gatekeepers and reach massive audiences. On the other hand, it risks reinforcing the very systems it seeks to change by making only surface modifications while leaving deeper structures intact.

In his Latinx Pop Culture class, Frederick identifies a similar dynamic in Ben Young's 2018 sci-fi film *Extinction*, which deserves more critical attention than it received. The film opens in familiar genre territory: Peter (Michael Peña), a blue-collar mechanic, struggles with prophetic visions of war in a near-future society under corporate control. The twist—that Peter is in fact a synthetic being and part of a hidden society resisting militarized human incursions—radically recasts the entire narrative framework. In its climactic reveal, *Extinction* constructs a Latinx-coded futurism where the presumed expendable laborer is actually a higher-order being: thinking, feeling, resisting, and protecting his family against human supremacist violence.

We both agree that *Extinction* ultimately urges all its viewers to reconsider racialized labor and the sci-fi trope of synthetic life through the lens of brown survival rather than alienation. The storyworld reframes brownness not as an obstacle to modernity, but as its ethical and evolutionary horizon. That this radical reimagining came and went with little fanfare speaks to how threatening such narratives remain to dominant culture.

Confronting Colonial Mythologies

The incremental insurgency performed in *The Mandalorian* strengthens considerably through its retooling of the Western's colonizer-Indigenous binary. This appears most clearly in the show's revolutionary treatment of the Tusken Raiders, a transformation that took forty years to achieve. In "Chapter 9: The Marshal," instead of rendering Tuskens as faceless savages (as they were in *A New Hope* [1977], functioning as pure racial terror), they are given cultural depth, complexity, and dignity.

They communicate through a fully developed sign language (created by deaf actor Troy Kotsur, who also played a Tusken). They possess deep territorial knowledge that proves essential for survival. They forge uneasy but mutually beneficial alliances with settlers—a rare nod to Indigenous sovereignty in a franchise long reliant on settler mythologies. The episode suggests that cooperation, not domination, ensures survival in harsh environments. This lesson feels particularly relevant as climate change forces us to reconsider Indigenous knowledge systems long dismissed by Western science.

This incremental insurgency gains momentum in *The Book of Boba Fett* (2021), which expands *The Mandalorian*'s Tusken Raider storyline, giving the Tuskens even more narrative space and cultural texture. We witness their rituals, technologies, and social bonds. We see Boba Fett—himself a figure of cultural hybridity—learn their ways, earn their trust, and undergo transformation to become one of them. For several episodes, the show offers *Star Wars*' most sustained and respectful engagement with Indigenous-coded cultures.

Limits of Representation

Truth be told, however, we were both shocked and profoundly troubled (and disappointed?) with the episode "Chapter 3: The Streets of Mos Espa" in *The Book of Boba Fett*, where we witness the aftermath of the tribe's massacre by the Kintan Striders, the Nikto speeder bike gang. On the one hand, it reconstructs the genocidal violence experienced by Indigenous communities globally. On the other hand, the genocidal violence is reduced to functioning as a plot device. The deeper representation is undercut by a genre-bound ending: The Tusken community is slaughtered, clearing narrative space for Fett's vengeance arc. The tribe exists primarily as a crucible for his transformation—granting him legitimacy and wisdom, then vanishing into the desert sand.

This resolution replicates a familiar settler-colonial cycle that haunts American genre fiction. Indigenous peoples are often framed as noble but doomed, repositories of ancient wisdom whose only narrative function is to ennoble white (or white-coded) protagonists before conveniently disappearing. Their deaths motivate the hero's journey but never constitute tragedy worthy of sustained mourning or structural change.

When Frederick asks his students to reflect on this episode and others, he connects it to what Gerald Vizenor calls "manifest manners"—the performance of respect for Indigenous cultures that masks their symbolic and literal erasure. Even when genre narratives attempt respectful representation, they often remain tethered to story structures that require Indigenous absence for the hero's presence.

So while we applaud *The Mandalorian* and *Boba Fett* as genuine attempts to push against decades of racist representation and decolonizing toxic masculinity, as long as Indigenous death functions only as a narrative tool and Latinx masculinities remain hidden behind masks, we question whether these efforts in fact only reinscribe the very patterns they seek to undo.

Beyond Apocalypse Tourism

The Mandalorian joins a vast catalogue of postapocalyptic narratives that imagine social collapse as adventure opportunity rather than lived trauma. From *The Walking Dead* (2010–2022) to *The Last of Us* (2023–), these stories center characters navigating devastated landscapes with resourcefulness and weapons, transforming catastrophe into entertainment for those who've never lived precarity. They offer apocalypse tourism—disaster voyeurism for the comfortable.

But for many Latinx communities, apocalypse isn't speculative—it's Tuesday. Frederick's students from Puerto Rico describe Hurricane Maria's aftermath in terms identical to disaster fiction: no power for months, no clean water, no government response, communities organizing survival through mutual aid while federal agencies failed them. Peter's family in California navigates fire seasons that turn skies apoc-

Figure 17 *The Walking Dead* (2010–2022) shows postapocalyptic landscapes as fiction, even when similar conditions are a reality for many people.

alyptic orange and air toxic, evacuation bags packed by the door from June through November. The border has been a militarized dystopia for decades, families separated by walls and policies that would seem heavy-handed in fiction. ICE raids create disappeared people with an efficiency that would make Imperial forces envious.

These lived experiences of ongoing catastrophe rarely inform apocalyptic fiction. Instead, mainstream media offers white preppers in luxury bunkers, lone wolves roaming wastelands, and nuclear families (literally) surviving through superior firepower and hoarded resources. The communal strategies that actually enable survival—mutual aid, resource sharing, collective care, community knowledge—get dismissed as weakness or relegated to background flavor. The protagonist never survives because their neighbors share food; they survive because they have more ammunition.

Undying of Zombie Ideologies

The Western genre refuses to die because it serves essential ideological functions: justifying conquest as progress, violence as necessity, and white supremacy as natural order. Even progressive revisions often maintain core structures while updating surface representation. *The Mandalorian* makes space opera from Western DNA but keeps the lone gunslinger, the frontier town, and the Indigenous threat that requires negotiation or elimination. The empire changes costumes but not structure.

The challenge for Latinx creators isn't avoiding the Western—its influence on American media makes that impossible, its tropes too deeply embedded in our narrative DNA. The challenge is transforming it from within. This requires more than casting brown faces in white roles or adding Spanish dialogue to English scripts. It demands reimagining fundamental assumptions about space, conflict, resolution, and survival itself.

If we're living through slow apocalypse—climate change, democratic breakdown, racial capitalism's death throes—*The Walking Dead* offers instructive metaphor, though not through its zombies. The show's vision of postcollapse society involves constant violence, resource scarcity, and trust breakdown. Communities that attempt cooperation are destroyed by those maintaining competition. The message broadcast across eleven seasons is clear: Only the violent inherit the earth. Kindness kills. Compassion is weakness. Trust is death.

But actual disaster response reveals opposite dynamics. When systems fail, communities organize mutual aid. When governments abandon populations, people create parallel care structures. When official channels close, informal networks open. The real walking dead aren't zombies but ideologies that insist only violence ensures survival, that care is weakness, that we must hoard rather than share. These ideologies shamble on despite mounting evidence of their failure.

The inadequate warning systems and delayed FEMA response to flooding in the Guadalupe River communities west of Frederick exemplify how real disasters unfold. It wasn't zombies that killed people—it was structural classism that placed vulnerable communities in flood zones, language barriers that prevented warning dissemination, and bureaucratic indifference that delayed rescue efforts. The heroes weren't gun-toting loners but neighbors with boats, churches that opened their doors, and informal networks that shared resources.

Latinx communities' responses to COVID-19 revealed these dynamics with crystalline clarity. Mutual aid networks distributed food and medicine when governments failed. Community health workers provided culturally competent care when hospitals turned people away. Extended families created pods balancing safety with connection when official guidance proved impossible to follow. These strategies emerged from long experience navigating state failure—skills developed through surviving previous apocalypses that mainstream America didn't notice.

What strikes us most is how these survival strategies get coded as "cultural" rather than recognized as advanced social technologies for collective survival. When white preppers stockpile goods, it's rugged individualism. When Latinx communities share resources, it's poverty. When wealthy families pod up, it's prudent. When immigrant families maintain multigenerational households, it's primitive. Coding reveals more about power than practice.

After the End, We Begin Again

If apocalypse is already here—unevenly distributed, playing out in slow motion—we need better stories about surviving it. Not through individual excellence or superior firepower but through collective care and communal innovation. Not by mourning lost civilization but by building new ones from available materials. Not through walls and weapons but through bridges and bonds. The future depends less on who has the most bullets than on who maintains the strongest communities.

In his scholarly work, Frederick writes about apocalyptic futurisms that refuse the dystopia-utopia binary. Drawing on Indigenous and Latinx knowledge systems that understand time as circular rather than linear, these futurisms imagine endings as beginnings, collapse as transformation, and death as transition to new forms of life. They don't minimize suffering but refuse to let it define horizons of possibility.

His latest graphic novel project exemplifies this approach. Set in 2045 L.A. after catastrophic climate collapse, it refuses disaster porn aesthetics. Instead of focusing on civilizational breakdown, it centers communities that adapted: floating neighborhoods in Marina del Rey built from reclaimed materials, vertical farms in Boyle Heights that feed thousands, Indigenous-led water reclamation in the San Fernando Valley that combines traditional knowledge with salvaged technology. The apocalypse happened, but so did survival, transformation, and moments of joy. Children still play in the ruins. People still fall in love. Communities still celebrate. Life finds ways.

Peter's current scripts explore similar territory in the medium of TV, crafting narratives that center Latinx communities navigating various apocalypses—both metaphorical and literal—through collective action rather than individual heroism. His work insists on the revolutionary potential of care networks, chosen families, and community resilience in the face of systemic collapse.

This Is the Way . . .

The Mandalorian succeeded partly because it arrived during our own apocalypse, offering escape into simpler conflicts with clearer resolutions. A masked hero felt suddenly relatable. But it also resonated because Din Djarin's journey—from isolation to connection, from violence to care, from individual survival to communal responsibility—mirrors what many discovered during lockdown. We need each other to survive. We protect the vulnerable because their survival ensures ours. We build families from whoever shows up because blood family might be locked down across closed borders.

These lessons feel revolutionary in Western contexts but reflect what marginalized communities have always known. The apocalypse isn't coming; it's been here, unevenly distributed, for generations. Those who survived previous ends carry wisdom essential for navigating current ones. The question isn't whether society will collapse but how we'll build from ruins. Not if we'll face catastrophe but how we'll care for each other through it.

Latinx futurisms don't deny difficulty or romanticize struggle. They insist that those who've survived conquest, slavery, genocide, and ongoing erasure possess knowledge essential for species survival. They imagine futures in which that knowledge centers rather than margins. They create mythologies in which we don't just survive apocalypse—we transform it into soil for new growth.

The Western may never die, but it can evolve. *The Mandalorian* points toward possibility—genres mixing and mutating, structures shifting under pressure, and old stories finding new forms. With Latinx creators at the helm rather than the margins, those possibilities expand exponentially. We don't need permission to imagine ourselves in futures. We're already here, masked or unmasked, building worlds from whatever materials remain.

The mask that hides Pedro Pascal's face becomes metaphor for larger patterns of visibility and erasure. But it also suggests that recognition can come through routes other than traditional representation. Sometimes we know heroes by their actions rather than their faces. Sometimes care speaks louder than dialogue. Sometimes the most radical act is not killing the enemy but raising the child.

As we write this, the pandemic continues its mutations, climate change accelerates, and democracy frays. The apocalypse continues, unevenly distributed but expanding. In this context, *The Mandalorian* offers not escape but instruction: survive through connection, resist through care, build family from fragments. The way forward isn't lonely heroism but collective survival. Not the Western's violent individualism but something newer and older—the communal strategies that helped our communities survive every previous ending.

This is the way. Not the way of the lone gunslinger but the way of the people who survive catastrophe through solidarity. Not the way of walls but the way of bridges. Not the way of hoarding but the way of sharing. The revolution isn't written in the stars. It begins in our unlearning—and relearning—how to feel, act, and live. It's a turning away from toxic, reflexive binaries and a turning toward compassion, nuance, and complexity.

Chapter 6

LATINX TEEN SHOWS

When Corina was a freshman in high school, she told Frederick over dinner one evening: "Mapa, my friends and I play a game where we count how many shows have someone who looks like us as the main character. We usually stop counting pretty quick." This impromptu sociology, teenagers building metrics for their own erasure, captures why teen TV matters so intensely. Teenhood is when identity crystallizes, when young people desperately seek mirrors and windows: mirrors to see themselves reflected, windows to imagine who they might become.

This simple counting game reveals a profound truth about representation and its psychological impact. When teenagers must actively search for themselves in media landscapes, when finding a single character who shares their background becomes a victory worth tallying, we witness the violence of erasure in real time. The game itself—its existence, its rules, its consistently disappointing outcomes—documents how Latinx teens learn early that mainstream culture considers them peripheral to the main story.

Teen Brains

Frederick is endlessly fascinated with teens, and not just because he lives with one. He constantly reads the research to understand this wondrous developmental phase. Like the phase from birth to six years old, adolescence (identified roughly as ages 13 to 18) is another huge moment in our physical, cognitive, and emotive development. It's a time when adrenal stress, sex, and growth hormones flood the brain. It's a time of physical and emotional awkwardness. It's a time of risk-taking. It's a time of explosive erotic attractions.

It's also a time of explosive curiosity and great creativity.

Teens generate novel ideas. They see solutions where others might not. Their brains are responsive and flexible. The teen's interfacing with abundant and novel experiences, stimulations, sensations, experimentations, and explorations leads to the formation of massive amounts of new neural pathways that in turn lead to learning new things.

This neurological flowering happens precisely when media consumption peaks. Teenagers spend more time with screens than any other age group, not from laziness but from developmental necessity. Their brains seek patterns, test identities, and imagine futures through narrative. The stories they consume during this neural explosion don't just entertain—they literally shape cognitive architecture. When those stories consistently exclude or stereotype Latinx teens, this absence creates its own neural pathways: ones that encode invisibility as normal, marginalization as natural.

Paradoxically, teenhood is both a time of great creativity (neural plasticity) and great vulnerability. It's a time when the brain's tremendous connectivity moves from the back to the front of the brain: the frontal and parietal lobes and prefrontal cortex—the rational or executive areas of the brain where language, impulse control, and prospective memory (holding in mind intention to act in the future) develop and gain interconnected neural complexity. It isn't until late-stage teenhood and early adulthood that we begin to see a more front-to-back, balanced brain connectivity.

Optimally, we need both the emotion and reason systems to work, and together.

This biological reality makes authentic representation urgent rather than optional. During the very years when teens are wiring their understanding of possibility, when they're forming the neural networks that will shape adult decision-making, media offers scripts for being. For white teens, the white-optic-constructed scripts proliferate endlessly—every genre, every platform, every narrative style offers multiple ways of existing. For Latinx teens, these white-optic-constructed media scripts remain limited: the gangster, corner drug dealer, maid's daughter, model minority with sellout assimilationist aspirations. These scripts straitjacket imaginations. They hardwire a narrow, often self-destructive range of future possibilities.

Of course, teen brains are shaped in real time and place; the way the teen executive brain is shaped varies according to the changes produced in time and place, and these changes are human made.

Today in the United States, we see the making of an education system and social tissue that's failing Black, Indigenous, and People of Color (BIPOC) teens. It's failing to provide the everyday conditions for the realization of their full potentialities—for the good life, or *eudaimonia* as Aristotle called it in his *Nicomachean Ethics*.

This failure extends beyond formal education into the cultural education provided by media. When Aristotle wrote about human flourishing, he emphasized the importance of models—examples of excellence that young people could emulate and adapt. Contemporary Latinx teens face a peculiar poverty: abundant media that rarely models their potential excellence. They see themselves as problems to be solved (the at-risk youth), burdens to be managed (the teen parent), or exceptions to be celebrated (the one who "makes it out"). Rarely do they see themselves as complex humans deserving of ordinary extraordinary stories.

Sex and sexuality remain a natural part of our development—yet taboos continue to silence this central ingredient in the teen coming-of-age experience, especially when it comes to same-sex and fluid sexual orientations, behaviors, and attractions. Indeed, while the research shows that same-sex sexual and nonfixed (asexual or bisexual, for instance) orientations are common, because of continued social stigmas, bullying, and homophobic violence, these general features of our development continue to be mostly hidden from sight in mainstream narrative representations.

Gender diverse, trans, nonbinary, gay, lesbian, and queer teens are stigmatized and discriminated against. They are also the victims of acts of violence. Life for LGBTQ+ teens is a constant presence of massive psychological stress loads. This can and does lead to negative psychological processes and outcomes such as anxiety, depression, self-harm, and even suicide.

The intersection of these marginalizations creates a nexus of interlocking systems of oppression that compound rather than simply add. For Latinx LGBTQ+ teens, this matrix operates through specific mechanisms: the machismo that polices gender expression, the Catholicism that condemns nonheterosexual desire, and the *familismo* that makes rejection devastating because family is everything.

LGBTQ+ teens of color navigate daily the compounded effects of rigid stereotypes about both sexuality and race. These experiences vary across racialized communities. For Black and Latinx teens, discrimination often comes from authority figures—police officers, teachers, and service industry workers. Asian American teens, on the other hand, are more likely to encounter racially motivated mistreatment from their peers, both in school and beyond. Across all groups, teen boys tend to be targeted more frequently than girls when it comes to racial discrimination.

We both agree that the white-optic televisual complex rarely captures the complexities of these specific pressures, instead defaulting to generic coming-out narratives that assume white, middle-class contexts.

Collective Daydreaming

It's not that science or practice says we need to shelter teens from stressors. It's that there are, say, good and bad stressors. Just as flight-or-fight cortisol release helped our ancestors out of those woolly mammoth attacks, a certain amount of stress today for teens can be useful. Teens need a healthy level of stressors to learn how to cope, problem-solve, and overcome everyday challenges. However, if faced with the onslaught of woolly mammoths *constantly*, teens suffer from attention deficit, information retention issues, and can develop self-destructive thoughts and behaviors.

This distinction between productive and destructive stress maps directly onto media representation. Good stress might be Corina seeing a character like her who faces challenges and overcomes them—modeling resilience and strategy. Bad stress is Corina never seeing characters like her, or seeing them only as victims, villains, or tokens.

The constant vigilance required to translate white-optic-constructed narratives into personal relevance, to imagine yourself into stories that exclude you, creates its own cortisol load for Latinx,

BIPOC, and LGBTQ+ teens. This is the woolly mammoth of representation: not a single dramatic encounter but the daily exhaustion of psychic labor.

We both know well that teens need the time and space for reflection and creativity. They need to be able to daydream. For disenfranchised teens especially, daydreams become an important space for creativity that's self-empowering, allowing them to imagine agency to act, engage, explore, and be curious, in a world that constantly seeks to control and surveil all their thoughts and actions. Indeed, the daydreaming brain is the wish-fulfillment brain that seeks peace from everyday assaults. It is the fiction-making brain.

With lots of work as well as skill-building and sharpening, creatives can focus their fiction-making brains in ways that produce remarkable narratives in the form of stories, novels, TikToks, animation, and film shorts—you name it. Frederick elsewhere calls this process the engaging of one's "will to style": the labor (focus and skill) in directing our fiction-making capacity to create something new in the world—in the universe.

Yet daydreaming requires raw material. The imagination doesn't create from nothing but recombines existing elements into new configurations. When Latinx teens lack diverse media representations, their daydreaming operates from scarcity. They must work harder to imagine themselves as protagonists, to envision futures beyond stereotypical constraints. This additional labor, the extra work of dreaming past absence, represents another hidden tax on marginalized youth.

For Latinx teens, white-optic-constructed televisual narratives have *not* created opportunities for co-daydreaming. Rather they've offered funhouse mirrors at best—distorted reflections that suggest Latinx teens exist only as problems to be solved or diversity quotas to be filled.

Peter knows this pressure from both sides. As a father, he watched his sons navigate media landscapes that alternately ignore and stereotype them. As a creator, he has fought countless battles to center young Latinx characters without reducing them to after-school-special lessons. The gap between what Latinx teens need and what Hollywood thinks they want reveals everything broken about youth media.

A Breakthrough from Tucson

The journey from recognition of absence to creation of presence requires both courage and opportunity. Peter's groundbreaking work represents one trajectory of this journey—from frustrated viewer to active creator, from counting absences to generating alternatives.

As mentioned earlier, Peter's *Greetings from Tucson* represented a watershed moment in Latinx teen representation. The cast alone signaled its ambitions: Lupe Ontiveros as the *abuela*, Teri Garr and Martin Mull as the Irish grandparents, Carmen Electra, Jeff Garlin, and Jacob Vargas, an actor Peter would go on to collaborate with repeatedly. The show also gave Aimee Garcia her start. For Peter, it was a thrilling convergence of talent that proved a Latinx family comedy could attract a deep ensemble and hold its own on The WB.

The significance of this casting went beyond individual performances. Ontiveros, already a legend from *Selena* (1997) and countless other roles, brought gravitas that signaled this wasn't disposable teen content. The multigenerational cast reflected how Latinx families actually function—not as nuclear units but as extended networks in which *abuelas* shape daily life as much as parents. The mix of established and emerging Latinx talent created mentorship opportunities rarely available in Hollywood's segregated spaces.

The show broke ground by centering a bicultural family without making that the entire plot. The Tiant family navigated typical teen issues—crushes, school pressure, sibling rivalry—while also dealing with the specific realities of being Mexican American in Arizona. The show let code-switching, bilingual puns, and cultural references stand without extensive explanation.

This trust represented a radical departure from Hollywood's usual treatment of Latinx content. No character stopped to explain why they called their grandmother "abuela." No very special episode taught white audiences about *quinceañeras*. The show assumed—correctly—that Latinx viewers deserved content that didn't other them through exposition, while non-Latinx viewers could keep up or catch up. This narrative confidence modeled how authentic representation works: not through educational asides but through lived normalcy.

Most significantly, the show's diversity wasn't performative; it was structural. When a WB casting executive called to remind shows to diversify their casts, Peter pointed out the absurdity: Six of his series regulars were Latinx, with one white woman. Did she want him to add more white people? The exchange exposed how "diversity" initiatives often assume whiteness as the default, requiring reminders to include others rather than centering them from conception.

Greetings from Tucson premiered alongside *George Lopez* (2002–2007), creating what should have been a breakthrough moment. At the American Latino Media Arts Awards that year, Peter celebrated Lopez's back-nine pickup with characteristic generosity, framing it as a collective victory: when one of us wins, we all win. Yet despite critical acclaim and a full-season order, *Greetings from Tucson* wasn't renewed, teaching early lessons about the precarity of Latinx representation.

The show's cancellation despite success established a pattern that continues today: Latinx shows must overperform to survive while white shows fail upward into multiple seasons. This economic discrimination creates cascading effects. Fewer shows mean fewer opportunities for Latinx writers, directors, and actors to build careers. Fewer careers mean fewer people in positions to greenlight future shows. The cycle perpetuates itself through structural rather than individual prejudice.

Disney's Latinx Paradox

The evolution from explicit representation in *Greetings from Tucson* to the coded presence in Disney's offerings reveals how corporate media often retreats from progress rather than advancing it. This regression teaches its own lessons about the politics of visibility.

As we mentioned earlier, *Wizards of Waverly Place* (2007–2012) succeeded almost despite itself. The Russo family was written half Mexican on Theresa's side and Italian American on Jerry's, but the show rarely sat with that specificity for long. Gomez's casting as Alex did the cultural heavy lifting, with generations of Latinx viewers claiming her as fan cultures formed in her wake.

Peter, who wrote for the show, remembers the delicate negotiations around Alex's identity. Network executives worried that making her "too ethnic" would limit appeal. But Gomez brought something ineffable—a way of moving through space, a particular humor, a specific

Figure 18 Selena Gomez brought an innate Latinidad to her *Wizards of Waverly Place* (2007–2012) character, Alex Russo, whose half Mexican heritage rarely got room to breathe.

warmth with family—that coded as Latinx to those looking for it. Young viewers picked up on microexpressions, on the way she said "Mom," on her particular brand of rebellion that felt culturally specific even when scripts remained generic.

This phenomenon—audiences reading identity through performance despite textual absence—demonstrates both resourcefulness and desperation. Latinx viewers became expert semioticians, parsing gesture and inflection for cultural connection. They did the work that writers wouldn't, filling narrative gaps with interpretive labor. While this creativity shows resilience, it also reveals failure: Audiences shouldn't have to imagine representation into existence.

The show's massive success—becoming Disney Channel's longest-running series—proved what creators knew: Authentic performance resonates even through colorblind writing. But it also revealed limitations. Alex rarely spoke Spanish, never mentioned cultural heritage, never addressed the complexity of being mixed (both magical and ethnic). She existed in that peculiar Disney space where difference is visible but never voiced.

This sanitized diversity became Disney's template: Cast inclusively but write generically. The strategy allows networks to claim representation while avoiding specificity that might challenge white viewers. It creates a peculiar kind of erasure—bodies present but cultures absent, faces visible but voices muted. For young Latinx viewers, this half-representation might be worse than absence, suggesting they can exist only by denying parts of themselves.

Modern Milestones

The streaming era initially promised to shatter broadcast TV's conservative constraints. Without advertising concerns or channel-surfing viewers to retain, platforms could supposedly serve niche audiences with authentic content. The reality proved more complex, as algorithmic recommendation systems and global market pressures created new forms of homogenization.

Netflix's *On My Block* (2018–2021) marked a seismic shift in Latinx teen representation. Set in the fictional Los Angeles neighborhood of Freeridge, the show centered four friends—Monse, Cesar, Ruby, and Jamal—navigating high school while dealing with gang violence, gentrification, and family deportation threats. The show refused to choose between comedy and tragedy, mixing both in ways that reflected real Latinx teen experiences.

This tonal complexity challenged Hollywood's tendency to segregate Latinx stories into either gritty social realism or broad comedy. Real life doesn't respect genre boundaries: families facing deportation still laugh at dinner, teens dodging gang recruitment still stress about school dances. *On My Block* captured this simultaneity, trusting audiences to hold multiple emotions without confusion. The show's success proved viewers craved complexity, not simplification.

Ruby Martinez (Jason Genao) became an instant icon—a nerdy, anxiety-ridden teen who spoke in telenovela-worthy declarations while organizing school dances with military precision. His *quinceañero* episode showcased how the show balanced specificity with universality. The cultural significance of the celebration wasn't explained for white audiences; instead, viewers witnessed Ruby's genuine emotion as he danced with his *abuela,* understanding through feeling rather than exposition.

Every Latinx teen character navigates code-switching, but few shows acknowledge its psychological toll. Characters slip between languages and cultures seamlessly, as if translation were frictionless. But real code-switching exhausts. It requires constant vigilance, continuous translation, and sustained performance of belonging in spaces that resist your presence.

We love the way the show moved beyond linguistic code-switching to show how Latinx teens portray code-switching identities in different contexts—and ultimately for survival. Ruby's attempts to fit into white spaces—his obsession with proper English, his anxiety about family embarrassment—revealed code-switching as survival strategy rather than skill, shifting between personas depending on context: tough in the streets, vulnerable at home, ambitious at school.

Peter pushed for storylines addressing this exhaustion in every show he worked on: the migraine from thinking in two languages all day, the muscle memory of straightening your spine in white spaces, the relief of dropping performance among family, until family demands its own performances. These mundane violences shape Latinx adolescence but rarely make it to the screen.

The absence of these stories creates its own damage. When media presents code-switching as effortless, real teens experiencing exhaustion feel weak rather than normal. They internalize structural violence as personal failure, thinking they should navigate multiple worlds without strain. Authentic representation would show the cost, validating the fatigue that comes from constant cultural translation.

And while we both champion Mindy Kaling's *Never Have I Ever* (2020–2023) as brilliantly centering a South Asian American teen experience, it falls far short in its Latinx representation. It's set in Southern California, where we are the majority population, yet there's a near-absence of Latinx characters. The show's Sherman Oaks setting couldn't justify this absence—the San Fernando Valley's demographics include substantial Latinx populations across economic strata. Yet there's a selective blindness at play when it comes to representing Latinx characters, perpetuating Latinx invisibility through narrative neglect.

It's like Chris Rock said at the Academy Awards one year, in so many words: if you live in L.A. and create a film without Latinxs, you are really working hard to ignore reality.

The frustration here isn't about competitive oppression but collaborative possibility. *Never Have I Ever* proved audiences' hunger for specific cultural stories told with intelligence and humor. Its success should have opened doors for similar Latinx-centered narratives. Instead, it reinforced Hollywood's tendency to treat minority representation as zero-sum, as if only one nonwhite story can exist at a time.

Hulu's *Love, Victor* (2020–2022) centered Victor Salazar, a Latinx teen navigating his sexuality while balancing family expectations and cultural pressures. Minutes in, it seems full of promise as a kind of Disney-PG-13 Latinx coming-out narrative. The voice-over narration drops us into the middle of the life of Victor Salazar (Michael Cimino). Among unpacked boxes with memorabilia from his life in Texas (flags, school-assignment drawings, and trophies), he's telling the viewer (us) what he's texting Simon Spier—yes, that fictional protagonist that headlined the first mainstream teen gay coming out flick, *Love, Simon* (2018). Victor congratulates Simon for coming out to students at Creekwood High. He also lets Simon know that coming out isn't so easy for everybody. Ten episodes later, and with much ado about a lot of teen romancing (mostly straight) in between, Victor finds the strength to own his queerness.

The initial couple of minutes just described set up certain viewer expectations. That Victor's coming out will be more complicated than Simon's because, well, he's Latinx. And certainly, as the show unfolds, we learn of the subtle ways that his *papá*, Armando (Mando) (James Martinez), is a *machista*. Indeed, Mando's many micro-*machista* turns of phrase and actions (especially directed at the *chavalito*, Mateo) are a second-generation, watered-down version of the *abuelo*, Tito's, outright destructive homophobia. Of course, we have *papás* just like Mando. Many of us were raised in Catholic families (lapsed or otherwise), like the Salazars, where talk of desire and sexuality is framed only in terms of straight coupling conventions. This promoting and naturalizing of heteropatriarchal conceptions of desire willfully ignore and violently excise from existence our LGBTQ+ brothers and sisters.

Frederick's beef with *Love, Victor* lies not with the writing of *machista* characters like Mando and his *papá*, Tito. It lies elsewhere. It lies in the lazy reconstructions of Latinidad, or Latinoness. After his ten-episode binge, he felt left wanting, like someone had tried to dupe him into feeling and thinking about characters that ultimately sell a neoliberal version of its "be true to yourself" message. It made him ponder: Have the showrunners, Isaac Aptaker and Elizabeth Berger (writers of *Love, Simon*), ever stepped out of their prophylactic protected biosphere into, well, the world?

The Authenticity Equation

The challenge of creating authentic Latinx teen content reveals deeper questions about who controls narrative and for whom stories are told. Each creative choice—from casting to dialogue to story arc—involves negotiations between authenticity and accessibility, specificity and universality.

A show that Peter wrote for, Netflix's *Mr. Iglesias* (2019–2020), took a different approach: explicit, proud, unapologetic Latinx identity in a high school setting. Gabriel Iglesias brought his stand-up persona to a fictional Wilson High School, playing a history teacher returning to his alma mater to inspire new generations. The show wore its heart on its sleeve—sometimes to a fault—but represented something crucial: Latinx adults investing in Latinx youth.

Peter served as the co-showrunner and fought for specific choices that defined the show's voice. Marisol (Cree Cicchino), the overachieving student who works nights to support her family, wasn't written as tragic but as powerful. Her exhaustion came from structural inequality, not personal failure. Her intelligence wasn't exceptional but expected—disrupting narratives in which smart Latinx kids are aberrations rather than norms.

This reframing from exceptional to expected challenges fundamental assumptions about Latinx youth. Too often, media presents academic achievement as surprising, as if Latinx teens succeed despite their culture rather than because of it. Peter's insistence on normalizing excellence refused this narrative violence. The smart kids in *Mr. Iglesias* weren't special; they were standard, suggesting a world where Latinx intelligence surprises no one.

The show's DNA embedded status reversals that reflected real high school dynamics. The white Advanced Placement History teacher (Oscar Nuñez) was passionate but ineffective. The football coach taught drama. The counselor needed more help than the students. These inversions weren't arbitrary: they reflected how marginalized students often navigate schools where authority doesn't equal wisdom.

Despite critical acclaim and Gabriel Iglesias's massive fan base, the show lasted only two seasons. We both still throw up our hands, less in disbelief and more with deep disappointment. Even when brown-optic teen shows get the ratings and numbers, they face extinction.

Familia, Mixed Status and in Flux

The contemporary moment presents particular challenges for representing Latinx teens. Immigration debates, economic precarity, and cultural transitions create contexts that demand nuanced storytelling.

Yet these same pressures often push media toward simplistic narratives that reinforce rather than complicate stereotypes.

While *Gentefied* (2020–2021) focused on twentysomething cousins, its portrayal of neighborhood teenagers revealed how gentrification shapes adolescent identity. The high school characters code-switched not just linguistically but economically—Instagram aesthetics at school, food truck realities at home. They navigated between worlds with a sophistication that adults rarely credit teenagers.

One episode followed teenage volunteers at Mama Fina's, the family's Boyle Heights taquería, revealing how gentrification creates generational divides even within families. The teens saw opportunity in change—new customers meant college funds—while adults saw cultural erasure. This complexity, which refused to offer simple villains or heroes, trusted young viewers to process nuance.

The show understood that gentrification isn't abstract policy but lived experience. For Latinx teens in changing neighborhoods, every day brings micronegotiations: Which friends can afford the new juice bar? Which families are getting pushed out? How do you maintain community when community itself becomes commodity? These ques-

Figure 19 Annie Gonzalez and J. J. Soria as Lidia Solis and Erik Morales in *Gentefied* (2020–2021).

tions shape identity as powerfully as any traditional coming-of-age marker.

Frederick teaches this episode alongside Latinx cultural studies and media scholarship to enhance appreciation of how brown-optic televisuals construct narratives that can capture vitally complex lived experiences, that can engage and invite Latinx teens into co-dreaming spaces.

As with *Mr. Iglesias,* when the show was canceled after two seasons, we sighed deeply, not out of disappointment, but out of pain. We felt vicariously how it was being punished for its complexity and refusal to gentrify this multigenerational Latinx narrative into a white-optic-shaped and consumable morality tale.

Revolutionary Normalcy

The radical move is letting marginalized lives just be ordinary. The power of casual representation—families eating dinner, teens stressing about tests, parents arguing about bills—lies in its refusal to justify existence through exceptionalism.

The *One Day at a Time* revival (2017–2020), another show Peter worked on, centered a Cuban American family with radical matter-of-factness. Elena's *quinceañera* episode became instant canon—not just for its portrayal of coming out in a Latinx family but for how it handled tradition, modernity, and the specific ways culture and sexuality intersect for young Latinas.

For us, this episode refused easy answers. Elena's rejection of traditional femininity wasn't presented as either betrayal or liberation, but as a complex negotiation with heritage. Her mother's struggle to accept both her daughter's sexuality and her rejection of cultural markers showed how progress happens in families—messily, painfully, incompletely. The resolution—Elena dancing with her chosen family after her father's rejection—honored both loss and possibility.

The show's Latinx teen characters—Elena and Alex—represented different responses to Cuban American identity. Elena, an intellectual and activist, challenged every tradition while secretly cherishing family bonds. Alex, popular and seemingly assimilated, revealed surprising depths of cultural connection. Neither was wrong; both were real.

The show refused to adjudicate between preservation and adaptation, showing both as valid survival strategies.

What made *One Day at a Time* revolutionary was its assumption of complexity. Teen characters discussed immigration policy at dinner, processed intergenerational trauma through humor, and navigated racial microaggressions at school without becoming "very special episodes." Their lives were political because Latinx existence is political, but they were also allowed to be silly, selfish, and seventeen.

For us, the show's premature cancellation and brief resurrection demonstrated both progress *and* precarity. Latinx fans mobilized and saved, showing the power of our community. Yet that it needed saving showed how little has changed in the white-optic media-industrial complex's attitudes toward Latinx content.

Nuevas Ondas

The newest wave of Latinx teen shows reflects both accumulated wisdom and persistent challenges. Creators build on previous successes while navigating new platforms' algorithmic demands. The results show evolution and repetition, breakthrough and retreat.

Netflix's *Freeridge* (2023), a spinoff of *On My Block*, shifted focus to a new group of teens in the same neighborhood. Centering female friendship—Gloria, Ines, Demi, and Cam—the show explored how Latinx teen girls navigate different pressures from those faced by their male counterparts. The supernatural element (a cursed box from a yard sale) provided metaphorical weight to real anxieties about family curses, generational trauma, and the feeling that forces beyond your control shape your destiny.

The show's single season highlighted the precarity of Latinx teen shows: canceled despite strong viewership and critical praise. Its premature end exemplified how streaming metrics favor broad appeal over dedicated audiences, punishing shows that serve specific communities well rather than general audiences adequately.

This cancellation logic reveals streaming's false promises. Platforms claimed to value niche audiences, to sustain shows broadcast couldn't support. Instead, they created new forms of precarity—shows easier to launch but quicker to cancel, success measured in global metrics that disadvantage culturally specific content. The infinite shelf space of streaming meant nothing if shows couldn't survive long enough to build mythology.

While *The Horror of Dolores Roach* (2023) primarily focused on adult Dolores, this Prime Video horror series included crucial flashbacks to her teen years, showing how systemic failures shape trajectory. Young Dolores, played by Justina Machado in flashbacks, navigated poverty, violence, and limited options with resilience that ultimately couldn't overcome structural barriers. The show's horror elements literalized what poverty does to bodies and souls, making visible the violence of neglect.

The Disney+ series *Ultra Violet & Black Scorpion* (2022) brought a Mexican American teen *lucha libre* superhero, Violet Rodriguez, to screens, explicitly connecting cultural identity to superhero mythology. Violet's powers come from Mexican wrestling legacy and Indigenous artifacts, making heritage the source of strength rather than an obstacle to overcome. The show's bilingual approach—characters switch between English and Spanish naturally—refused to slow down for monolingual viewers.

These recent shows demonstrate both learning and forgetting. They build on their predecessors' innovations while facing the identical structural barriers. Each cancellation resets progress, forcing the next creators to re-prove what previous shows already demonstrated: that Latinx audiences exist, that specificity attracts rather than repels viewers, and that authentic representation succeeds creatively and commercially.

The Streaming Squeeze

The streaming era promised infinite space for niche content, including authentic Latinx teen shows. Instead it created new forms of precarity. Shows get greenlit more easily but are canceled faster. Two seasons became the new norm, barely enough time to build mythology or deepen character. The algorithm's hunger for immediate engagement punishes slow builds and complex narratives.

Peter has watched multiple Latinx-centered teen projects die in development because streaming services can't figure out how to market them. They want the authenticity that brings critical acclaim but fear the specificity that might limit the audience. What emerges is sanitized diversity—shows that look inclusive in promotional materials but center white perspectives in actual episodes.

The mathematics of streaming work against Latinx content. Global platforms need global hits, but cultural specificity reads as limitation rather than strength. Marketing departments struggle with shows that they can't reduce to universal themes. The paradox: Platforms want "authentic diverse voices" but only if those voices speak in ways everyone understands. This impossibility—be specific but universal, be authentic but accessible—traps creators in unwinnable negotiations.

The economics are brutal. Latinx teen shows get smaller budgets, less marketing, and lower cancellation thresholds than white equivalents. Then executives point to "underperformance" to justify not greenlighting similar projects. The cycle continues: Less investment leads to less viewership, which leads to less investment.

Brown-Optic Infrastructures

While traditional TV fails them, Latinx teens build their own media ecosystems on TikTok, YouTube, and Instagram. Creators like Yaritza Diaz and Diego Ramirez produce content that gets millions of views without ever pitching to networks. They perform sketches about strict Latinx parents, first-generation college stress, and cultural inside jokes that would never survive a network notes session.

Frederick has his students lean into these platforms in their weekly class assignments, where his students create sophisticated storymaking and storytelling in these short formats. Sixty-second Instagram Reels and TikToks contain complete narratives with callbacks to previous videos, creating serialized content without traditional distribution. Comment sections become writers' rooms where audiences suggest storylines and creators respond in real time.

These digital natives understand something TV executives don't: Specificity is strength. The more particular their content—the more it speaks to exact experiences of being Guatemalan in Georgia or Salvadoran in San Francisco—the more it resonates. They've proven what Hollywood doubts: Millions of people connect with stories about navigating *quinceañera* planning while parents work three jobs, about translating school documents because you're the only English speaker, about being both too Mexican for school and too American for family gatherings.

These young, vital creators bypass gatekeepers entirely, building audiences that dwarf cable viewership. They monetize through sponsors and merchandise rather than advertising breaks. Most importantly, they maintain creative control—no executives demand they make content more "universal." They succeed through specificity, building global audiences for extremely particular experiences.

The revolution seems to be happening on phones, not screens. While the media-industrial complex continues to gatekeep Latinx stories, Latinx teens are creating content that reaches millions globally. They prove daily what executives deny: Authenticity attracts audiences, specificity creates connection, and Latinx teens hunger for their own stories told their own way.

Coming-of-Age Complexities

The fundamental problem with Latinx teen representation isn't just a matter of quantity but of narrative framework. Coming-of-age stories assume movement from ignorance to knowledge, dependence to independence, ethnicity to assimilation. But what if Latinx teens aren't coming of age but are already aged by navigating multiple worlds? What if the story isn't growing up but growing sideways—expanding rather than ascending?

Frederick proposes something akin to lateral development narratives that resist linear progression. Characters who become more themselves rather than less; who deepen cultural connections while expanding horizons; who reject the binary of traditional versus modern by creating third spaces. These stories exist in our communities but struggle to reach screens shaped by Western development models.

This narrative innovation requires rethinking basic assumptions about growth. Western coming-of-age stories often frame culture as something to overcome—the protagonist must leave home to find themselves. But for many Latinx teens, finding themselves means diving deeper into their heritage while simultaneously creating new cultural forms. They remix rather than reject, creating identities that are both/and rather than either/or.

We recognize the trap in demanding perfect representation from the few Latinx teen shows that exist. No single show can capture the diversity of Latinx adolescence—urban and rural, documented and undocumented, Spanish-dominant and English-only, Indigenous and mestizo, island and mainland. The solution isn't perfect, but it shows abundant options.

Yet as Peter has argued until blue in the face, abundance requires structural change. More Latinx writers in rooms, but also as showrunners in these rooms. More Latinx directors helming episodes, but also entire series. More Latinx executives greenlighting shows, not just consulting on them. The pipeline from page to screen needs reconstruction, not just diversification.

New Voices, New Hopes

Despite frustrations, both of us remain hopeful. Frederick's University of Texas at Austin students create media that centers their experiences without apology. As one of these students, Corina expects representation and critiques its absence with sharp intelligence.

The hallway test Corina described is changing. Shows like *Diary of a Future President* (2020–2021), *The Expanding Universe of Ashley Garcia* (2020), and *Julie and the Phantoms* (2020) centered young Latinas navigating complex worlds before their cancellations. They weren't perfect—perfection isn't the goal—but they existed. Each creates space for more.

Recent additions like Disney+'s *Saturdays* (2023), which focuses on BIPOC teens navigating divorced parents and roller-skating culture, show an evolution in storytelling. The show treats multicultural friendship as default, not diversity achievement. Characters speak multiple languages, navigate multiple homes, and honor multiple traditions without any of it being the "problem" of the episode.

The revolution happens in these accumulating instances—narrative moments that together form movements. A teen show in which kids speak Spanglish without subtitles. A protagonist who prays to Virgen de Guadalupe without explanation. A family dinner where everyone talks over one another in multiple languages, with no one translating for the audience. These moments accumulate into mirrors where Latinx teens finally see themselves clearly.

As we've both seen in our creative and learning spaces, small victories matter because representation is cumulative. Each authentic moment makes the next one possible. Each show that succeeds by centering rather than including Latinx teens makes it harder for executives to claim such shows can't work. The argument shifts from whether to how, from if to when.

Hallway Tests No More

Latinx teen shows matter because adolescence is when invisibility hurts most. When you're figuring out who you are, absence suggests you don't exist. When you're imagining who you might become, stereotypes suggest limited possibilities. Authentic representation doesn't just reflect, it projects, offering futures worth growing toward.

The shows discussed here—successful and canceled, revolutionary and problematic—map an evolution from accidental inclusion to intentional centering. But evolution isn't enough. Revolution requires treating Latinx teens as the default rather than a deviation, as centered rather than a special interest.

The cognitive science is clear: The stories we consume during adolescence shape neural pathways that influence lifelong patterns of thought and possibility. For Latinx teens consuming media that either erases or stereotypes them, these patterns encode limitation. But authentic representation can encode expansion—showing multiple ways of being Latinx, teenage, and human simultaneously.

Corina no longer plays the hallway test. Not because she's a too-serious college student now, nor because representation is perfect. She doesn't play it now because she's tired of measuring her existence against others' imaginations. She creates her own media, finds creators who center her, and demands better from what exists. Her impatience is instructive: Why should she wait for Hollywood to discover what she's always known?

That's the future: not begging for inclusion but assuming belonging, not counting representations but creating them, not growing up invisible but growing up so visible that invisibility becomes unimaginable. The neural pathways that form during adolescence—shaped by stories seen and unseen—determine not just individual futures but collective possibilities. Every authentic representation creates new synaptic connections, new ways of being in the world. Every erasure reinforces old limitations.

The revolution isn't coming. It's already happening, and by teens of color who refuse to wait for permission to exist fully. They dream themselves into being through TikToks and Instagram Reels, through fanfic and YouTube channels, through group chats and Discord servers. They build the mirrors they need, understanding that reflection isn't passive but active, not just seeing but creating what deserves to be seen.

This self-creation through digital media represents more than individual empowerment—it's collective world-building. Each Latinx teen who posts their truth makes it easier for another to do the same. They create networks of authenticity that bypass Hollywood's gatekeepers entirely. Their metrics of success—views, likes, shares, but also comments like "this is exactly my life"—prove what TV executives deny: Specificity connects rather than alienates.

The future of Latinx teen representation may not run through Hollywood at all. It may emerge from bedrooms and phones, from teens who've given up on waiting for permission. They create the representation they need, building audiences Hollywood claimed didn't exist. In doing so, they prove the ultimate truth: Latinx teens don't need Hollywood to validate their existence. Hollywood needs them to remain relevant.

Their impatience is revolution. Their creativity is resistance. Their visibility—self-generated, collectively amplified, impossibly diverse—creates the future by living it now. They understand what Frederick and Peter have spent careers fighting for: Representation isn't charity or political correctness or market expansion. It's recognition of what already exists, acknowledgment of who has always been here, invitation to stories that have always been worth telling.

The hallway test ends not when Hollywood provides enough representation but when Latinx teens stop looking to Hollywood for validation. That future is already here, created one TikTok, one web series, one group chat at a time. The revolution will not be televised because it doesn't need TV. It needs only the tools to tell stories and the courage to insist that those stories matter. Both are abundant.

The future is now.

Chapter 7

OUR TOP LATINX TV SHOWS

"We should make a list," Frederick suggested during one of our video calls, both of us exhausted from analyzing representation failures. "Our top Latinx TV shows. The ones that actually mattered."

Peter laughed. "You realize we'll never agree, right? And everyone will hate our choices?"

He was right, of course. Creating canons is political work, especially for communities whose contributions have been systematically erased. Every inclusion implies exclusions. Every ranking suggests hierarchies. Yet the exercise felt necessary—not to create definitive truth but to map the territory of Latinx TV, to honor what's been achieved while acknowledging how far we have to go.

What emerged from our debates wasn't just a list but a conversation about value, impact, and the different ways representation matters. Some shows broke ground. Others broke hearts. Many did both. All revealed the complex negotiations Latinx creators and characters navigate in an industry that alternately fetishizes and erases us.

1. *I Love Lucy* (1951–1957)

We begin at the beginning, though the beginning itself is complicated. *I Love Lucy* gave us Desi Arnaz as Ricky Ricardo—a Cuban bandleader married to a white woman, speaking Spanish on primetime TV, succeeding through talent rather than assimilation. For 1950s America, this was revolutionary. That the show remains beloved seventy years later testifies to its foundational impact.

But Frederick teaches *I Love Lucy* with necessary complexity. Yes, Desi Arnaz was a pioneer who fought for creative control, invented the rerun, and built a production empire. But Ricky Ricardo was also a stereotype—hot-tempered, malaprop-spouting, and perpetually frustrated by his wife's schemes. The show's humor often derived from his accent, his "Latin temper," his otherness in white America.

Peter's grandmother watched *I Love Lucy* religiously, finding joy in seeing someone who looked like her husband on screen. But his immigrant father, coming of age in the 1960s, saw Ricky differently—as a limitation, a caricature that employers and teachers expected him to either embody or explicitly reject. Both responses are valid. Both are true. The show opened doors while installing frames that still constrain us.

What *I Love Lucy* established was the template for Latinx inclusion in American TV: We could belong if we were entertaining, if we married white, if we succeeded in approved ways, if our difference provided comedy rather than challenge. Every subsequent show negotiates with this template, either reproducing or resisting it.

2. *Chico and the Man* (1974–1978)

Freddie Prinze was twenty when *Chico and the Man* premiered, making him one of the youngest stars in TV history. His Chico Rodriguez was revolutionary—a young Chicano who was smart, funny, ambitious, and unapologetically Mexican American. He didn't code-switch for comfort. He challenged Ed Brown's gruff racism with humor that had an edge. He represented possibility.

The show's premise—generational and racial conflict resolved through reluctant partnership—feels formulaic now. But in 1974, seeing a young Latino man as co-lead rather than sidekick, as a solution rather than a problem, was groundbreaking. Prinze brought complexity to what could have been caricature, insisting on Chico's full humanity even when scripts reduced him to catchphrases.

Frederick can't teach *Chico and the Man* without discussing Prinze's suicide in 1977. The pressures of being *the first*, of carrying community representation, of navigating Hollywood's racism while barely out of adolescence—these killed as surely as the bullet. The show continued briefly with a child character replacing Chico, but the heart was gone. Prinze's death became a cautionary tale about the cost of breakthrough.

Yet the show's impact persists. Peter grew up hearing his father quote Chico's "Looking good!" as affirmation and armor. A generation of Chicano comedians cites Prinze, a Puerto Rican playing Chicano, as both inspiration and warning. The show proved Latinx leads could carry series, attract audiences, and create cultural phenomena. That Hollywood learned the wrong lessons—focusing on Prinze's tragedy rather than his talent—doesn't diminish his achievement.

3. *Miami Vice* (1984–1989)

Miami Vice might seem like a strange inclusion: a show created by white producers, centered on white cops, famous for pastel suits and Phil Collins songs. But the show's Miami was unprecedentedly Latin, not just in setting but in sensibility. Spanish wasn't translated. Latinx characters weren't explained. The city's Caribbean and Latin American connections drove plots rather than providing an exotic backdrop.

Edward James Olmos's Lieutenant Martin Castillo embodied a different Latinx masculinity than TV had seen. Silent where stereotypes demanded volubility, controlled where clichés required passion, and mystical yet technological, Castillo confused categories. His backstory is connected to CIA operations in Southeast Asia and Latin America, making him a walking critique of American imperialism even while serving its local apparatus.

Figure 20 *Miami Vice* (1984–1989) not only established a whole fashion scene in the 1980s but also depicted Miami in an unadulterated manner.

The show's aesthetic—neon and noir, tropical and technological—created a visual language for representing Miami that persists today. But more importantly, it normalized Latinx presence in the American imagination. Characters spoke Spanish without subtitles. Santería priests provided crucial information. Colombian cartel members had complex motivations. The representation wasn't always positive, but it was present, persistent, and unexplained.

Peter worked with several *Miami Vice* alumni who described the show's production as genuinely multicultural. Latinx crew members influenced everything from location choices to dialogue authenticity. The show's success proved that deeply local, culturally specific stories could achieve global reach—a lesson TV keeps forgetting and rediscovering.

4. *Resurrection Blvd.* (2000–2002)

Resurrection Blvd. represented a watershed—the first English-language drama series centered entirely on a Latinx family. The Santiago family of East Los Angeles navigated boxing, gentrification, sexuality, and tradition across three seasons that felt simultaneously too short and perfectly complete. The show let complex family dynamics unfold without anthropological scaffolding for outsiders.

What made *Resurrection Blvd.* special was its refusal to be special. The Santiagos weren't standing in for all Latinx families or teaching white audiences about Mexican American culture. They were specific people in a specific place dealing with specific challenges. The boxing subplot—forced by network executives who couldn't imagine Latinx drama without sports or crime—became a metaphor for fighting larger battles.

Frederick shows episodes in his media classes to demonstrate ensemble storytelling—*avant la lettre.* No single character carries representational weight because all share it. The father's traditionalism, the son's sexuality, the daughter's ambition, the mother's strength—each gets full development rather than serving others' arcs. The show modeled what Latinx TV could be with sufficient resources and creative control.

The show's cancellation after three seasons, despite critical acclaim, established a pattern that continues: Latinx shows must overperform to survive while white shows get multiple seasons to find audiences. But *Resurrection Blvd.*'s DNA persists in every subsequent family drama that centers brownness without apology.

5. *George Lopez* (2002–2007)

George Lopez succeeded where many failed by centering working-class Mexican American life without condescension or tragedy. George's job at Powers Brothers Aviation grounded storylines in economic reality. His mother Benny's harsh parenting reflected survival strategies rather than cultural pathology. His wife Angie's whiteness created opportunities for cultural negotiation without dominating narratives.

The show's humor emerged from specificity—the plastic on the furniture, the beans in the freezer, the *chancla* as discipline—that resonated across Latinx communities while remaining accessible to broader audiences. Lopez insisted on writers' room diversity, bringing in voices who understood these references firsthand, not from research.

Peter appreciates how the show handled bilingualism. Characters code-switched naturally, with Spanish appearing for emphasis, emotion, or exclusion. The audience learned to read context rather than requiring translation. This trust in viewers' intelligence opened space for other shows to assume multilingual competence.

But for both of us, the show also revealed limitations. George's dysfunction often stemmed from his Mexican American identity rather than universal human flaws. His mother's harshness got played for laughs rather than examined as intergenerational trauma. The show's need to be relatable sometimes flattened complexity into stereotype. Still, for six seasons, the Lopez family occupied prime network real estate, proving Latinx families could anchor mainstream success.

6. *Ugly Betty* (2006–2010)

Ugly Betty's adaptation of the Colombian telenovela *Yo soy Betty, la fea* (1999–2001) became a cultural phenom that transcended its premise. America Ferrera's Betty Suarez wasn't just navigating the fashion world's cruelty but representing first-generation professional aspirations. Her family—immigration-status-complicated father, traditionally feminine sister, flamboyant nephew—provided grounding while she climbed Manhattan's ladder.

The show's genius lay in using telenovela aesthetics—heightened emotion, dramatic reveals, camp sensibility—within American dramedy structure. This wasn't translation but transformation, creating a new genre that honored both traditions. Betty's journey from Queens to Manhattan became a metaphor for bicultural navigation, complete with code-switching, family obligations, and imposter syndrome.

Frederick teaches *Ugly Betty* as a watershed for Latinx feminine representation. Betty was neither spicy Latina nor suffering saint, but an ambitious professional whose ethnicity informed without defining her. Her relationship with her family stayed central throughout, rejecting narratives suggesting success requires severing cultural ties. When she chose to leave *Mode* for London, it was expansion rather than escape.

The show's four-season run proved that Latinx-centered stories could attract broad audiences, launch careers, and create cultural impact. That it took a Colombian telenovela to achieve this—rather than an original American creation—reveals persistent industry blindness to domestic Latinx stories.

7. *Jane the Virgin* (2014–2019)

Jane the Virgin achieved something extraordinary—it made telenovela structure legible to American audiences while honoring its roots. The show's narrator, speaking in Spanish-accented English, guided viewers through twists with affection rather than mockery. Jane's virginity premise could have been conservative moralizing, but became an exploration of choice, desire, and agency.

Gina Rodriguez's Jane Villanueva represented a new kind of Latina protagonist—educated, ambitious, sexual (despite virginity), and deeply rooted in family and culture. Her conversations with her mother and grandmother, conducted in Spanish and English without pattern, reflected real multilingual family dynamics. The show trusted audiences to follow without translation, normalizing bilingualism in prime time.

What elevated *Jane the Virgin* beyond a clever premise was its emotional authenticity. Jane's struggles—single motherhood, career ambition, romantic confusion, family obligation—felt real despite telenovela heightening. The show's magical realism, from animated hearts to dramatic music stings, externalized internal experience rather than mocking it.

Peter admires how showrunner Jennie Snyder Urman, though not Latina, built a writers' room that centered Latinx voices and experiences. The show's specificity—Venezuelan telenovelas, Miami Latinx culture, immigration complexity—emerged from lived experience rather than research. This collaboration model, with white showrunners actively centering marginalized voices, offers one path toward better representation.

8. *One Day at a Time* (2017–2020)

The Netflix and then Pop TV revival of *One Day at a Time* represented everything TV could be with sufficient care, craft, and cultural competence. Gloria Calderón Kellett and Mike Royce created a show that was specifically Cuban American and universally resonant, politically engaged and hilariously funny, traditional in structure and radical in content.

Every episode balanced multiple perspectives without false equivalence. When Elena came out, the show honored both her truth and her grandmother's struggle to understand. When Schneider revealed his addiction, it connected to Penelope's post-traumatic stress disorder and medication resistance. The personal was always political, but politics emerged from character rather than lecture.

Frederick uses the show to teach about "thick description" (per Clifford Geertz) in media—representation that includes texture, contradiction, and complexity rather than flattening into types. The Alvarez family practiced Catholicism and Santería, valued tradition and progress, spoke Spanish and English in patterns that revealed relationship dynamics. No single character represented "the Latinx perspective" because the show understood there's no such thing.

The show's cancellation despite critical acclaim and a devoted fan base revealed the limitations of streaming. Netflix's algorithm couldn't capture communal viewing, social media engagement, or depth of connection. When Pop TV rescued it for a fourth season, it proved that some shows matter beyond metrics—but also that the industry rarely recognizes this value.

9. *Gentefied* (2020–2021)

Gentefied arrived at the perfect moment, when conversations about gentrification, authenticity, and cultural preservation dominated Latinx discourse. The show's three cousins—Erik the activist intellectual, Chris the aspiring chef, Ana the queer artist—represented different responses to neighborhood change. None were wrong. All were complicated. The show refused simple villains or heroes.

What made *Gentefied* revolutionary was its assumption of Latinx centrality. The show didn't explain *quinceañeras*, translate Spanish, or provide anthropological context. It assumed viewers either knew or would learn, either belonged or would visit respectfully. This confidence in its own perspective created space for complexity, impossible when constantly translating for imagined white audiences.

Peter worked with several *Gentefied* writers who described the freedom of centering brownness without apology. Story discussions could focus on emotional truth rather than cultural education. The show's two-season run felt too brief but also complete—it said what it needed to about this moment in Latinx life without overstaying or overexplaining.

10. *Los Espookys* (2019–2022)

Los Espookys deserves inclusion for sheer audacity. The show's refusal to make sense in conventional terms—mixing horror, comedy, surrealism, and telenovela without explanation—created something genuinely new. Its characters were weird, not because they were Latinx but because they were weird. Their Latinidad was fact, not feature.

The show's creators—Julio Torres, Ana Fabrega, and Fred Armisen—built a world where queerness, strangeness, and brownness coexisted without conflict. Characters spoke Spanish and English without any pattern. Plots involved demon possession and parking tickets with equal seriousness. The show asked audiences to feel, not decode.

Frederick teaches *Los Espookys* as an example of "postrepresentation" media—work that assumes inclusion rather than arguing for it. The show's cancellation surprised no one; it was too strange for algorithmic success. But its existence proved that Latinx creators, given freedom, will create beyond existing categories.

List as Living Document

We both acknowledge that our list is a snapshot, not scripture. Our criteria shifted through discussion—from pure quality to cultural impact, from representation metrics to emotional resonance. We surprised ourselves with agreements and enlightened each other through disagreements. In many ways, our conversation mattered more than the conclusions. Ultimately, too, when a new show drops—and we're hopeful that the new-generation creators tucked under Peter's wing will break new ground—the periodic table of great Latinx shows shifts. The next generation, like Corina, isn't satisfied with breakthroughs—they expect belonging.

Yet, these kinds of lists matter, and existentially. They honor labor, create memory, and insist on presence in spaces that practice erasure. Our list represents thousands of actors, writers, directors, and crew members who fought for authentic representation. They model different storytelling strategies. They prove that brown-optic narratives can succeed commercially while maintaining rich, vital cultural integrity.

And they remind us how much work remains. Ten shows across seventy years of TV is insulting scarcity. That we could create this list at all is an achievement; that it's so short is an indictment. The solution isn't more lists but more shows, more creators, more executives, more power.

Chapter 8

OUR TOP FIVE LATINX FILMS

"Five films?" Peter asked incredulously during our planning call. "Just five? To represent all of Latinx cinema?"

Frederick laughed. "I know. It's like asking someone to pick their five favorite family members. Impossible and slightly offensive."

But the constraint forced clarity. In narrowing from hundreds to five, we had to articulate values, weigh impact against artistry, and consider audience against authenticity. The resulting list—and the debate about it—revealed how Latinx cinema has evolved, where it's stuck, and why certain films become touchstones while others fade despite quality.

Before diving into selections, we must address the mammoth in the room: Our list skews heavily masculine. This isn't preference but symptom—Latinx cinema, like all cinema, has historically centered male stories, directors, and perspectives. The infrastructure of film production, from financing to festival selection, privileges masculine narratives while marginalizing feminine ones.

This doesn't excuse our selection but contextualizes it. Films like *Real Women Have Curves* (2002), *Mosquita y Mari* (2012), and recent entries like *Blast Beat* (2020) beautifully center nonmasculine perspectives. The pattern is undeniable: Latinx cinema, as canonized and remembered, skews heavily male. Arguably, this isn't individual failure but structural reality. Film financing, festival programming, critical attention, and cultural memory all privilege masculine narratives. Women directors like Patricia Cardoso, Aurora Guerrero, Janicza Bravo, Cecilia Aldarondo, and Patricia Riggen, among others, create essential work that struggles to receive equal recognition. The problem compounds when considering intersection with other identities. Where are the films centering queer Latinx experience beyond subtext? Where are the stories of Afro-Latinx and mestizo Indigenous Latinx life beyond stereotype? They exist—in shorts, documentaries, and independent features—but rarely achieve the platform or permanence of masculine narratives.

Our five films represent one possible canon, but alternative selections would be equally valid. A feminist canon might center the previously mentioned *Real Women Have Curves*, *Girlfight* (2000), *Mosquita y Mari*, as well as other extraordinary films like *The Chambermaid* (2022) and *Madres* (2021). A Latinx LGBTQ+ canon could highlight *La Mission* (2009), *Gun Hill Road* (2011), *The Garden Left Behind* (2019), and *We the Animals* (2018).

Regional canons matter too. New York Latinx cinema (*Raising Victor Vargas* [2002], *In the Heights* [2021], and *I Like It Like That* [1994]) differs from Los Angeles (*Mi Familia* [1995], *Quinceañera* [2006], and *A Better Life* [2011]), which differs from Texas (*Selena* [1997], *Lone Star* [1996], and *The Long Game* [2023]). Each region develops distinct aesthetics, concerns, and communities. National canonization obscures these specificities.

The point isn't choosing the correct canon but recognizing canonization as a political process. Every list makes arguments about value, impact, and identity. Our five films argue for historical importance, crossover success, and creative control. Other lists would make different arguments, equally necessary.

1. *El Norte* (1983)

Gregory Nava's *El Norte* remains the essential Latinx film—not because it's perfect but because it's foundational. The story of Rosa and Enrique Xuncax fleeing Guatemala's genocide for imagined American prosperity captures migration's complexity without romanticism or demonization. It's simultaneously specific (Mayan protagonists, Guatemalan civil war) and universal (displacement, aspiration, disillusion).

The film's structure—three parts representing Guatemala, Mexico, and the United States—maps both physical and psychological journeys. The Guatemala section grounds characters in beauty and violence, showing what they're forced to leave. Mexico becomes purgatory, neither home nor destination. The United States offers material possibility and spiritual death, dreams realized as nightmares.

Frederick teaches the film's famous scene where Rosa, dying from pesticide exposure, hallucinates her village while lying in a Los Angeles hospital. The sequence epitomizes magical realism's political potential—not escapist fantasy but revelation of how trauma, memory, and displacement create multiple realities. Students who've never migrated recognize the feeling of being simultaneously present and absent.

Peter remembers seeing *El Norte* in college and feeling seen in ways Hollywood films never allowed. The protagonists weren't criminals or saints but complex humans navigating impossible circumstances. Their Indigenous identity wasn't folklore but lived reality. Their tragedy wasn't inevitable but structural, caused by specific political and economic forces rather than cultural destiny.

The film's restoration and re-release by the Academy Film Archive speaks to its enduring relevance. Forty years later, its themes—forced migration, Indigenous persecution, American dream as nightmare—feel more urgent than ever. That it took decades for the Academy to recognize its importance reveals how Latinx films get relegated to sociology rather than recognized as art.

2. *La Bamba* (1987)

Luis Valdez's *La Bamba* achieved what seemed impossible: a Chicano story that crossed over without selling out. The Ritchie Valens biopic could have been a standard music tragedy—talented kid rises fast, dies young. Instead, Valdez crafted a meditation on family, identity, and the price of American success for brown bodies.

The film's genius lies in its refusal to translate. When Bob and Ritchie fight, they code-switch naturally between English and Spanish, revealing how language maps emotion. The family parties feel authentic because they are—Valdez cast actual families, used real locations, and refused to translate the cultural context. This specificity created universality; viewers recognized their own families regardless of ethnicity.

Lou Diamond Phillips and Esai Morales originally auditioned for opposite roles: Phillips for Bob, Morales for Ritchie. The resulting switch revealed a deep understanding of character dynamics. Ritchie's assimilation required the specific vulnerability that Phillips embodied. Bob's rage needed Morales's intensity. The casting switch transformed good performances into iconic ones.

Figure 21 Lou Diamond Phillips brings cultural complexity to his portrayal of Chicano rock star Ritchie Valens in *La Bamba* (1987).

Elizabeth Peña's Rosie Morales deserves particular recognition. In a film dominated by brother dynamics, she carved out space for feminine agency. Her confrontation with Bob about his treatment wasn't just relationship drama but a feminist assertion. Peña brought dignity to a role that could have been thankless, creating full humanity in limited screen time.

The film's box office success—over $52 million on a $6.5 million budget—proved what executives claimed impossible: Latinx stories could attract massive audiences. That Hollywood learned the wrong lesson—greenlighting more biopics rather than more Chicano stories—doesn't diminish Valdez's achievement.

3. *American Me* (1992)

Edward James Olmos's directorial debut, *American Me*, remains controversial thirty years later—which is exactly why it matters. The film's unflinching examination of Chicano gang culture, prison violence, and cyclical trauma refused easy answers or comfortable distance. Olmos played Montoya Santana not as a hero or villain but as a product of systems designed to create exactly such men.

The film's opening—the Zoot Suit Riots intercut with Santana's conception through rape—establishes how historical violence creates personal trauma. This isn't metaphor but methodology: State violence against communities produces violence within communities. The film traces this genealogy without excusing individual choices, holding both systemic and personal responsibility in tension.

What distinguished *American Me* from contemporaneous hood films was its refusal of redemption narratives. Santana doesn't find God, love doesn't save him, and violence doesn't provide meaning. The film's bleakness serves a purpose—to show how certain trajectories, once begun, resist Hollywood endings. This honesty cost Olmos professionally but created artwork that endures.

Frederick uses the film to discuss the double bind of representation. *American Me* was criticized for reinforcing stereotypes about Chicano criminality. But sanitizing gang reality would be a different dishonesty. The solution isn't avoiding difficult stories but ensuring they're not the only stories told. One film can't carry the entire community's representation—expecting it to creates impossible burden.

Peter admires Olmos's formal ambition. The film's visual language, influenced by Mexican muralism and German expressionism, creates beauty from brutality. Prison cells become canvases, bodies become landscapes, and violence becomes choreography. This aesthetic sophistication challenges assumptions about who can create "art cinema" versus "genre film."

4. *Mi Vida Loca* (1993)

Allison Anders's *Mi Vida Loca* stands as our list's essential feminine counterpoint—though calling it "counterpoint" reinforces the marginalization it challenges. The film centers young Latinas in Echo Park navigating gang life, motherhood, friendship, and survival. Anders, though white, spent years in the community, listening rather than imposing, learning rather than teaching.

The film's structure—multiple perspectives on interconnected events—refuses single-protagonist dominance. Each young woman gets her moment of centrality; her story told from her perspective. This multiplicity challenges both Hollywood narrative conventions and gang film traditions that center masculine authority. The homegirls aren't supporting players in male dramas but protagonists of their own.

Giggles' return from prison structures the film's feminist revelation. Her speech about not letting men divide homegirls isn't preachy but practical—survival wisdom earned through experience. The film shows how patriarchy operates within marginalized communities, how masculine violence depends on feminine division, and how solidarity offers alternative power.

The casting brought authenticity through community involvement. Many actors were local residents playing versions of themselves. This wasn't exploitation but collaboration—Anders shared profits, maintained relationships, and centered community voices in promotion. The film's cult following among Latinas testifies to the power of representation when done with respect.

That Anders directed this story raises necessary questions about authorship and authenticity. Can outsiders tell insider stories? The answer depends on approach: Anders listened, collaborated, and centered community voices over her own vision. Her success created the space for insider directors, while her mistakes showed why such space matters.

5. *From Dusk Till Dawn* (1996)

Our final selection sparked the most debate. *From Dusk Till Dawn* isn't obviously "Latinx cinema"—it's Robert Rodriguez directing Quentin Tarantino's script, featuring George Clooney and Harvey Keitel. But the film represents a crucial evolution: Latinx creative control over mainstream genre entertainment.

The film's structure brilliantly enacts this transition. The first half is pure Tarantino—criminal brothers on the run, hostage family, Mexican border as escape route. It's familiar American genre territory with Mexico as a backdrop. Then Salma Hayek appears as Santanico Pandemonium, performs the most iconic dance in 1990s cinema, and literally devours the white characters. The film transforms into Rodriguez's vision—vampires, Aztec mythology, and brown heroes saving the day.

This isn't a subtle metaphor. The white criminals who see Mexico as a lawless playground for their fantasies get consumed by the country's actual power. The survivors must ally with Mexican characters, respect Indigenous knowledge, and abandon American exceptional-

Figure 22 George Clooney stars as Seth Gecko in Robert Rodriguez's *From Dusk Till Dawn* (1996).

ism to survive. Rodriguez smuggled radical politics into exploitation packaging.

Hayek's performance deserves analysis beyond its surface sexuality. Yes, the dance caters to the male gaze—but then she kills everyone gazing. Her transformation from object to subject, from entertainment to threat, mirrors how Hollywood sees Latinx talent. We're welcome as decoration but dangerous with agency. Hayek and Rodriguez understood this, creating a scene that both serves and subverts expectation.

The film's success—$25 million domestic on a $19 million budget—proved Rodriguez's viability as a mainstream director while maintaining a distinctive voice. His ability to blend Mexican horror traditions with American genre expectations created a new cinematic language. That he did this while platform-building for other Latinx talent makes it revolutionary.

The Films We Carry

Our five brown-optic-created films—*El Norte, La Bamba, American Me, Mi Vida Loca, From Dusk Till Dawn*—represent different strategies for survival and success. They prove Latinx stories can achieve critical acclaim, commercial success, and cultural impact. They model approaches from social realism to genre transformation, from community collaboration to individual vision.

But they also reveal limitations. Made over forty years, they show how slowly progress comes and how easily it reverses. Each breakthrough film should have opened floodgates; instead they became exceptions that proved rules. The white-optic media-industrial complex treats each success as anomaly rather than evidence.

Yet we carry these films with us. They live in memory, in reference, in inspiration for what's possible. They created moments of collective recognition, theaters full of brown faces seeing themselves centered. They proved our stories matter to audiences that industry executives claimed didn't exist.

The next five films that matter might be streaming on phones, projected in community centers, or shared through networks we haven't imagined. They will certainly center stories these five couldn't tell, voices these five couldn't amplify.

As Latinx scholars, creators, and community members, our work is ensuring those films get made, seen, and remembered. The canon is never closed. The list is never final. The only failure would be stopping at five, at fifty, at any number that suggests we've told enough stories.

CODA

The Last Word Is Really the First

As we write this Coda, Frederick stands at his writing desk in his Latinx Pop Lab on the University of Texas at Austin campus. Across the room stands a 3-D printer, bookshelves filled with Black, Indigenous, and People of Color comics, and scholarly books that explore Latinx representation. Peter writes from his Los Angeles home, taking breaks between script notes and phone calls with industry executives. We're separated by geography but united in purpose: imagining futures where Latinx stories don't need special pleading or strategic justification to exist.

This book began as a podcast, a dialogue between scholar and practitioner, between analysis and creation. It evolved into something larger: an initial mapping of an expansive, multicontoured territory, a documentation of struggle, a celebration of achievement, and most importantly, a blueprint for transformation. We've traced the evolution from Lucy and Ricky's sanitized dynamic to the raw complexity of *Gentefied.* We've analyzed how the neo-Western transforms brown bodies into regenerative obstacles, and how the willful use of generic conventions can create resilient, resistant, and vital brown-optic-shaped narratives that decolonize minds, bodies, and actions. We've celebrated the brown-optic-shaped sci-fi that imagines us as agents in the positive transformation of the future.

And then, as we were putting the finishing touches on this manuscript, the biggest stage in American media proved our point for us. On February 8, 2026, Bad Bunny headlined the Super Bowl LX halftime show: about fourteen minutes, almost entirely in Spanish, 128 million viewers. No subtitles, no bilingual compromise, no network-mandated code-switch. Peter, who has spent decades hearing executives ask, "But will it play in Kansas?" finally had a definitive answer: 128 million people tuned in, and nobody changed the channel. What made the performance matter for everything we've argued in this book isn't just that a Latino artist stood at the center of American pop culture. It's that he *authored* it. Bad Bunny didn't show up to perform inside somebody else's vision. He built the world—every set piece, every musical choice, every refusal to translate—and dared the largest simultaneous audience in the country to meet him on his terms. That's the difference between presence and power, between being included and being in charge. Everything we've been saying about the white-optic media-industrial complex—who greenlights, who controls the pipeline, who decides what "universal" looks like—Bad Bunny answered by simply bypassing the question.

And here's the part that connects directly to what we said in the Introduction about digital disruptions and battles for narrative space: Within minutes of the halftime's final note, the performance shattered into a thousand TikToks, Instagram Reels, and reaction videos that reached audiences far beyond the broadcast. The memes, the debates, the analyses—they became their own ecosystem, proving that when Latinx creators exercise full authorial control over a narrative, the audience doesn't just consume it. They *inhabit* it, remix it, carry it forward. That's the infrastructure we've been talking about, not the kind built by studio executives in corner offices but the kind built by creators and communities who refuse to wait for permission. Not only did the performance stop Frederick in his tracks (he was finishing the last sentences for his *Latinx TV* book for Routledge), but he watched his daughter and her pals from the University of Texas at Austin sitting on the living room couch, dissecting the performance in real-time before the fourth quarter even started. Peter got texts from showrunner friends saying, "This is the pitch meeting I've been trying to have for twenty years." If this book is a blueprint, Bad Bunny's halftime show is the proof of concept: Latinx stories, told on Latinx terms, don't need to be translated to travel. They just need to be *unleashed.*

But documentation isn't destination. The real work—the work that keeps both of us up at night and gets us up in the morning—is building infrastructure for stories not yet told.

We titled this book *Two Vatos Talk Pop Cultura: Latinx TV, Film, and Futures Unscripted,* but it's really about Latinx future: who gets to imagine them, inhabit them, and profit from them. Every story that centers our communities creates space for more. Every authentic representation makes erasure harder to maintain. Every success proves what we've always known: Our stories matter, our voices resonate, and our visions expand what American media can become.

Corina doesn't ask whether Latinx characters belong in narratives. She asks why anyone imagines stories without them. She creates Instagram Reels that seamlessly blend English, Spanish, and visual storytelling, reaching audiences that Hollywood claims don't exist. She writes fanfic and creates TikToks centering mixed Mexipina (Mexican and Filipina) protagonists saving universes, leading revolutions, and finding love without tragedy. She expects more because she's seen enough to know scarcity isn't natural but manufactured.

Meanwhile, Peter's children, with college in their rearview mirrors, navigate professional worlds with sophisticated media literacy. They've developed analysis frameworks without formal training, calling out colorism, critiquing capitalist assumptions, and demanding queer representation as baseline. They create alternative canons through Discord servers and Instagram stories, building community around shows that center their experiences while righteously dismissing those that don't.

This generation terrifies and thrills us. They terrify because they won't accept the incremental progress we've learned to celebrate. They thrill because their impatience might actually break the systems we've only managed to crack.

La lucha sigue—the struggle continues. But so does *la creatividad, la comunidad, y la esperanza.* The struggle, the creativity, the community, and the hope.

The last word isn't ending but invitation: What story will you tell? What future will you imagine? What conversation will you begin?

The screen awaits. The page beckons. The audience gathers.

Órale, let's go.

TIMELINE

Latinx Media Milestones

1950s

- 1951: *I Love Lucy* premieres with Desi Arnaz as Ricky Ricardo, the first Latino lead in American TV.
- 1954: *Salt of the Earth* is released, a blacklisted film about the Mexican American miners' strike.

1960s

- 1962: Rita Moreno wins an Oscar for *West Side Story* (1961), the first Latina to win an Academy Award.
- 1965: Luis Valdez founds El Teatro Campesino, a revolutionary Chicano theater group.

1970s

- 1974: *Chico and the Man* debuts with Freddie Prinze as a breakthrough Latino lead.
- 1977: Freddie Prinze's death at twenty-two highlights the pressures of representation.
- 1979: *Boulevard Nights* is released, an early Chicano gang film.

1980s

- 1981: *Zoot Suit* becomes the first Chicano play adapted for film.
- 1983: *El Norte* is released, defining immigration narrative.
- 1984: *Miami Vice* premieres, featuring Edward James Olmos.
- 1987: *La Bamba* achieves crossover success.
- 1988: *Stand and Deliver* makes Edward James Olmos an educational icon.

1990s

- 1992: *American Me*, directed by Edward James Olmos, examines Chicano incarceration.
- 1993: *Mi Vida Loca* centers young Latinas in a gang narrative.

- 1995: *My Family/Mi Familia* spans three generations of Mexican Americans.
- 1996: *From Dusk Till Dawn* marks Robert Rodriguez's Hollywood arrival.
- 1997: *Selena* launches Jennifer Lopez's film career.

2000s

- 2000: *Resurrection Blvd.* becomes the first English-language drama series about a Latinx family.
- 2002: *Real Women Have Curves* celebrates Chicana body positivity.
- 2002: *Frida* brings Frida Kahlo's story to mainstream audiences.
- 2002–2007: *George Lopez* runs for six seasons on ABC.
- 2006–2010: *Ugly Betty* adapts the telenovela for American TV.
- 2007: America Ferrera wins a Golden Globe for *Ugly Betty*, the first Latina ever to do so.
- 2007–2012: *Wizards of Waverly Place* makes Selena Gomez a star.

2010s

- 2013: *East Los High* becomes the first English-language series with an all-Latinx cast, on Hulu.
- 2013: Robert Rodriguez launches El Rey Network, the first English-language Latinx-themed cable network (founded 2013; ceased linear broadcast 2021).
- 2014: *Jane the Virgin* premieres on The CW; Gina Rodriguez wins a Golden Globe for Best Actress in a Comedy, only the second Latina ever to win the award, after America Ferrera for *Ugly Betty* in 2007.
- 2014: Jorge R. Gutiérrez's *The Book of Life* brings Día de los Muertos to an animated feature film.
- 2015: *Hamilton* opens on Broadway, with Lin-Manuel Miranda rewriting the American founding narrative through hip-hop and a cast of color.
- 2016: *Elena of Avalor* debuts as Disney's first Latina princess.
- 2017: *Coco* becomes Pixar's first film centered on a Latinx family and Mexican culture; it wins the Academy Award for Best Animated Feature.
- 2017: "Despacito" (Luis Fonsi ft. Daddy Yankee) becomes the most-streamed song in history, marking Latin music's mainstream crossover dominance.

- 2017–2020: *One Day at a Time* reboot reimagines Norman Lear's classic with a Cuban American family, tackling immigration, queerness, and veteran post-traumatic stress disorder.
- 2018–2020: *Vida* premieres on STARZ with an all-Latinx writers' room, centering queer Chicana sisters in a gentrifying Boyle Heights.
- 2018–2021: *On My Block* centers Latinx and Black teens navigating life in an inner-city L.A. neighborhood.
- 2019: *Los Espookys*, co-created by Julio Torres, Fred Armisen, and Ana Fabrega, becomes HBO's first Spanish-language series.

2020s

- 2020–2021: *Gentefied* on Netflix explores gentrification in Boyle Heights through a Chicanx lens; America Ferrera executive produces.
- 2021: *In the Heights*, adapted from Lin-Manuel Miranda and Quiara Alegría Hudes's Tony-winning musical, brings Washington Heights to the big screen, sparking important debates about Afro-Latinx representation.
- 2021: *Encanto* becomes the first Walt Disney Animation Studios musical centered on a Latinx family (Colombian), winning the Academy Award for Best Animated Feature; "We Don't Talk About Bruno" tops the Billboard Hot 100.
- 2021: Jorge Gutiérrez's *Maya and the Three* reimagines Mesoamerican mythology as epic fantasy on Netflix.
- 2021: Steven Spielberg's *West Side Story* remake casts Ariana DeBose, who wins the Oscar for Best Supporting Actress, and gives Rita Moreno a new role sixty years after her original win.
- 2022: Jenna Ortega stars in *Wednesday*, which becomes Netflix's most-watched English-language series at the time of its debut.
- 2023: *Blue Beetle*, directed by Ángel Manuel Soto and starring Xolo Maridueña, becomes the first major-studio (DC) live-action superhero film to star a Latino lead.
- 2023: Eva Longoria's directorial debut, *Flamin' Hot*, brings a Latinx entrepreneurial narrative to mainstream audiences on Hulu and Disney+.
- 2024: The Latino Donor Collaborative's Latinos in Media report estimates the entertainment industry loses $12 to $18 billion annually due to insufficient Latinx representation.

- 2025: Pedro Pascal continues as one of Hollywood's most bankable stars across *The Last of Us* (season 2), *The Mandalorian*, and *Gladiator II*, marking an unprecedented run for a Latino leading man in prestige franchises.
- 2026: Bad Bunny headlines the Super Bowl LX halftime show, the first *reggaetonero* to do so, signaling Latin urban music's full arrival at the center of American popular culture.

FURTHER READING

Introduction: Two Vatos Walk into a Cultural Revolution

Aldama, Frederick Luis, ed. *Latinos and Narrative Media: Participation and Portrayal*. Palgrave Macmillan, 2013.

Aldama, Frederick Luis, ed. *The Routledge Companion to Latina/o Popular Culture*. Routledge, 2016.

Aldama, Frederick Luis, and Christopher González. *Latinx Studies: The Key Concepts*. Routledge, 2018.

Aldama, Frederick Luis, and William Anthony Nericcio. *Talking #browntv: Latinas and Latinos on the Screen*. The Ohio State University Press, 2019.

Beltrán, Mary C. *Latina/o Stars in U.S. Eyes: The Making and Meanings of Film and TV Stardom*. University of Illinois Press, 2009.

Fojas, Camilla. *Border Bandits: Hollywood on the Southern Frontier*. University of Texas Press, 2008.

García Canclini, Néstor. *Hybrid Cultures: Strategies for Entering and Leaving Modernity*. Translated by Christopher L. Chiappari and Silvia L. López. University of Minnesota Press, 1995.

Gray, Herman. *Watching Race: Television and the Struggle for Blackness*. University of Minnesota Press, 1995.

Mignolo, Walter D., and Rolando Vázquez. "Decolonial AestheSis: Colonial wounds / Decolonial Healings." *Social Text Online*, July 15, 2013, socialtextjournal.org/periscope_article/decolonial-aesthesis-colonial-woundsdecolonial-healings/.

Ortiz, Fernando. *Cuban Counterpoint: Tobacco and Sugar*. Translated by Harris de Onís. Duke University Press, 1995.

Perez, Domino Renee, and Rachel González-Martin, eds. *Race and Cultural Practice in Popular Culture*. Rutgers University Press, 2018.

Vargas, Deborah R., Lawrence La Fountain-Stokes, and Nancy Raquel Mirabal, eds. *Keywords for Latina/o Studies*. NYU Press, 2017.

Warner, Kristen J. *The Cultural Politics of Colorblind TV Casting*. Routledge, 2015.

Williams, Raymond. *Culture and Society, 1780–1950*. Columbia University Press, 1958.

Chapter 1: Diversity, Equity, and Inclusion in the Era of Blockbuster Superheroes

Aldama, Frederick Luis. *Latinx Superheroes in Mainstream Comics*. University of Arizona Press, 2017.

Andes, Stephen J. C. *Zorro's Shadow: How a Mexican Legend Became America's First Superhero*. Chicago Review Press, 2020.

Beltrán, Mary, and Camilla Fojas. *Mixed Race Hollywood*. NYU Press, 2008.

Hartman, Saidiya. *Lose Your Mother: A Journey Along the Atlantic Slave Route*. Farrar, Straus and Giroux, 2007.

hooks, bell. "Choosing the Margin as a Space of Radical Openness." In *Yearning: Race, Gender, and Cultural Politics*, 145–53. South End Press, 1990.

Muñoz, José Esteban. *Cruising Utopia: The Then and There of Queer Futurity*. NYU Press, 2009.

Negrón-Muntaner, Frances, Chelsea Abbas, Luis Figueroa, and Samuel Robson. *The Latino Media Gap: A Report on the State of Latinos in U.S. Media*. Columbia University, The Center for the Study of Ethnicity and Race, 2014.

Ramírez Berg, Charles. *Latino Images in Film: Stereotypes, Subversion, and Resistance.* University of Texas Press, 2002.
Said, Edward W. *Orientalism.* Pantheon Books, 1978.

Chapter 2: Ideal Versus Real Audiences

Aldama, Frederick Luis. *The Cinema of Robert Rodriguez.* University of Texas Press, 2014.
Aldama, Frederick Luis, ed. *Latinx TV in the Twenty-First Century.* University of Arizona Press, 2022.
Aldama, Frederick Luis, ed. *Latinx Fandoms.* University of Arizona Press, 2027.
Anzaldúa, Gloria. *The Gloria Anzaldúa Reader.* Edited by AnaLouise Keating. Duke University Press, 2009.
Beltrán, Mary. *Latino TV: A History.* NYU Press, 2022.
Boffone, Trevor, ed. *TikTok Cultures in the United States.* Routledge, 2022.
Case, Ariana, Katherine Pieper, and Stacy L. Smith. *Hispanic/Latino Representation in Film: Erasure On Screen & Behind the Camera Across 1,600 Popular Movies.* USC Annenberg Inclusion Initiative, 2023. https://assets.uscannenberg.org/docs/aii_11.3_hisp_latino_study_07-22.pdf.
Dávila, Arlene. *Latino Spin: Public Image and the Whitewashing of Race.* New York University Press, 2008.
Molina-Guzmán, Isabel. *Latinas and Latinos on TV: Colorblind Comedy in the Post-Racial Network Era.* University of Arizona Press, 2018.
Nielsen. *Hispanic Audiences in Focus: Trust in Media—The Key Factor Driving the Shift to Streaming.* Diverse Intelligence Series, 2023. www.nielsen.com/insights/2023/hispanic-audiences-in-focus-trust-in-media-the-key-factor-driving-the-shift-to-streaming/.
Rafele, Antonio, William Anthony Nericcio, and Frederick Luis Aldama. *Cultural Studies in the Digital Age: An Anthology of 21st Century Interdisciplinary Inquiries, Postulations, and Findings.* San Diego State University Press, 2021.

Chapter 3: Latinx Narco Narratives and the Neo-Western

Aldama, Frederick Luis, and William Anthony Nericcio. *Talking #browntv: Latinas and Latinos on the Screen.* The Ohio State University Press, 2019.
Benavides, O. Hugo. *Drugs, Thugs, and Divas: Telenovelas and Narco-Dramas in Latin America.* University of Texas Press, 2008.
Macías, Anthony. *Chicano-Chicana Americana: Pop Culture Pluralism Starring Anthony Quinn, Katy Jurado, Robert Beltran, and Lupe Ontiveros.* University of Arizona Press, 2023.
Rashotte, Ryan. *Narco Cinema: Sex, Drugs, and Banda Music in Mexico's B-Filmography.* Palgrave Macmillan, 2015.
Ruiz, Jason. *Narcomedia: Latinidad, Popular Culture, and America's War on Drugs.* University of Texas Press, 2023.

Chapter 4: Latinx in Sci-fi

Aldama, Frederick Luis, and Christopher González. *Reel Latinxs: Representation in U.S. Film and TV.* University of Arizona Press, 2019.
Dillon, Grace L., ed. *Walking the Clouds: An Anthology of Indigenous Science Fiction.* University of Arizona Press, 2012.
Duncan, Scott Russell, and Jenny Irizary, eds. *Xicanxfuturism: Gritos for Tomorrow.* Riot of Roses Publishing House LLC, 2025.

González, Christopher. *Galactic Herencia: Latinos in the Star Wars Universe.* University of Arizona Press, 2027.
Goodwin, Matthew David. *The Latinx Files: Race, Migration, and Space Aliens.* Rutgers University Press, 2021.
Merla-Watson, Cathryn Josefina, and B. V. Olguín, eds. *Altermundos: Latin@ Speculative Literature, Film, and Popular Culture.* UCLA Chicano Studies Research Center Press, 2017.
Noriega, Chon, Maya Montañez Smukler, and Nicole Ucedo, eds. *Science Fiction Against the Margins: Cinematic Futures, Global Imaginaries.* UCLA Chicano Studies Research Center Press, 2025.
Ramírez, Catherine S. "Deus ex Machina: Tradition, Technology, and the Chicanafuturist Art of Marion C. Martinez." *Aztlán: A Journal of Chicano Studies* 29, no. 2 (2004): 55–92.
Ramírez Berg, Charles. *Latino Images in Film: Stereotypes, Subversion, and Resistance.* University of Texas Press, 2002.

Chapter 5: Living the Apocalypse

Aldama, Arturo J., and Frederick Luis Aldama, eds. *Decolonizing Latinx Masculinities.* University of Arizona Press, 2020.
Córdoba, Antonio, and Emily A. Maguire, eds. *Posthumanism and Latin(x) American Science Fiction.* Springer International Publishing, 2023.
Nyong'o, Tavia. *Black Apocalypse: Afrofuturism at the End of the World.* University of California Press, 2025.
Saldarriaga, Patricia, and Emy Manini. *Infected Empires: Decolonizing Zombies.* Rutgers University Press, 2022.
Saldarriaga, Patricia, and Emy Manini. *Monsters vs. Patriarchy: Toxic Imagination in Global Horror Cinema.* Rutgers University Press, 2025.
Venditto, David. *Whiteness at the End of the World: Race in Post-Apocalyptic Cinema.* State University of New York Press, 2022.
Vizenor, Gerald. *Manifest Manners: Postindian Warriors of Survivance.* Wesleyan University Press, 1994.

Chapter 6: Latinx Teen Shows

Aldama, Frederick Luis, ed. *The Routledge Companion to Latino/a Popular Culture.* Routledge, 2016.
Boffone, Trevor, and Cristina Herrera. *Latinx Teens: U.S. Popular Culture on the Page, Stage, and Screen.* University of Arizona Press, 2022.
Boffone, Trevor, and Cristina Herrera, eds. *Atravesados: Essays on Queer Latinx Young Adult Literature.* University Press of Mississippi, 2025.
Kohnen, Melanie. *Queer Representation, Visibility, and Race in American Film and Television: Screening the Closet.* Routledge, 2015.
Molina-Guzmán, Isabel. *Dangerous Curves: Latina Bodies in the Media.* NYU Press, 2010.
Perez, Domino Renee. *Fatherhood in the Borderlands: A Daughter's Slow Approach.* University of Texas Press, 2022.
Valdivia, Angharad N. *Latina/os and the Media.* Polity Press, 2010.

Chapter 7: Our Top Latinx TV Shows

Aldama, Frederick Luis, ed. *Latinx TV in the Twenty-First Century.* University of Arizona Press, 2022.

Alvarez, Luis. *Chicanx Utopias: Pop Culture and the Politics of the Possible*. University of Texas Press, 2022.
Cepeda, María, and Dolores Inés Casillas, eds. *The Routledge Companion to Latina/o Media*. Routledge, 2016.
Geertz, Clifford. *The Interpretation of Cultures: Selected Essays*. Basic Books, 1973.
Rodríguez, Clara E., ed. *Latin Looks: Images of Latinas and Latinos in the U.S. Media*. Westview Press, 1997.

Chapter 8: Our Top Five Latinx Films

Aldama, Frederick Luis, ed. *Latinx Ciné in the Twenty-First Century*. University of Arizona Press, 2019.
Fregoso, Rosa Linda. *The Bronze Screen: Chicana and Chicano Film Culture*. University of Minnesota Press, 1993.
Fregoso, Rosa Linda. *MeXicana Encounters: The Making of Social Identities on the Borderlands*. University of California Press, 2003.
Noriega, Chon, ed. *Chicanos and Film: Representation and Resistance*. University of Minnesota Press, 1992.
Noriega, Chon A., and Ana M. López. *The Ethnic Eye: Latino Media Arts*. University of Minnesota Press, 1996.

FURTHER FILM VIEWING

A Better Life (Chris Weitz, 2011)
Alita: Battle Angel (Robert Rodriguez, 2019)
American Me (Edward James Olmos, 1992)
Amexicano (Matthew Bonifacio, 2007)
Ant-Man (Peyton Reed, 2015)
Ant-Man and the Wasp (Peyton Reed, 2018)
Avatar (James Cameron, 2009)
A Walk in the Clouds (Alfonso Arau, 1995)
Baby Driver (Edgar Wright, 2017)
Bad Teacher (Jake Kasdan, 2011)
Black Panther (Ryan Coogler, 2018)
Black Widow (Cate Shortland, 2021)
Blue Beetle (Ángel Manuel Soto, 2023)
Bread and Roses (Ken Loach, 2000)
Captain America: Brave New World (Julius Onah, 2025)
Carne y Arena (Alejandro González Iñárritu, 2017)
Center Stage (Nicholas Hytner, 2000)
Cesar Chavez (Diego Luna, 2014)
Coco (Lee Unkrich, 2017)
Colombiana (Olivier Megaton, 2011)
Crossing Over (Wayne Kramer, 2009)
Desierto (Jonás Cuarón, 2015)
Después del terremoto (Lourdes Portillo, 1979)
District 9 (Neill Blomkamp, 2009)
Doctor Strange in the Multiverse of Madness (Sam Raimi, 2022)
El Cantante (Leon Ichaso, 2006/2007)
El Mariachi (Robert Rodriguez, 1993)
El Norte (Gregory Nava, 1983)
El Super (Leon Ichaso, 1979)
Elysium (Neill Blomkamp, 2013)
Emilia Pérez (Jacques Audiard, 2024)
Empire (Franc. Reyes, 2002)
Extinction (Ben Young, 2018)
Extra Terrestres (Carla Cavina, 2016)
Fantastic Four (Tim Story, 2005)
Fast and Furious franchise (2001–)
Girlfight (Karyn Kusama, 2000)
Guardians of the Galaxy (James Gunn, 2014)
How to Be a Latin Lover (Ken Marino, 2017)
I Am Joaquin (Luis Valdez, 1969)
I Like It Like That (Darnell Martin, 1994)
Instructions Not Included (Eugenio Derbez, 2013)
In the Heights (Jon M. Chu, 2021)
It's a Disaster (Todd Berger, 2012)
Kids (Larry Clark, 1995)

Kingdom of Shadows (Bernardo Ruiz, 2015)
La Bamba (Luis Valdez, 1987)
La Mission (Peter Bratt, 2009)
Latinos Beyond Reel (Miguel Picker and Chyng Sun, 2013)
Live by Night (Ben Affleck, 2016)
Logan (James Mangold, 2017)
Lowriders (Ricardo de Montreuil, 2016)
Machete (Robert Rodriguez, 2010)
Machete Kills (Robert Rodriguez, 2013)
McFarland, USA (Niki Caro, 2015)
Memories of a Penitent Heart (Cecilia Aldarondo, 2016)
Mi Familia / My Family (Gregory Nava, 1995)
Mi Vida Loca / My Crazy Life (Allison Anders, 1993)
Nina (Cynthia Mort, 2016)
No Country for Old Men (Coen Brothers, 2007)
Nueba Yol (Ángel Muñiz, 1995)
Paranoid (John Duigan, 2000)
Paranormal Activity: The Marked Ones (Christopher B. Landon, 2014)
Piñero (Leon Ichaso, 2001)
Purgatorio: A Journey into the Heart of the Border (Rodrigo Reyes, 2013)
Raising Victor Vargas (Peter Sollett, 2002)
Real Women Have Curves (Patricia Cardoso, 2002)
Seguin (Jesús Treviño, 1981)
Selena (Gregory Nava, 1997)
Shang-Chi and the Legend of the Ten Rings (Destin Daniel Cretton, 2021)
Sicario (Denis Villeneuve, 2015)
Since I Laid Eyes (Adel L. Morales, 2014)
Sin City (Robert Rodriguez, 2005)
Singing My Way to Freedom (Paul Espinosa, 2018)
Sin Nombre (Cary Joji Fukunaga, 2009)
Sleep Dealer (Alex Rivera, 2008)
Stand and Deliver (Ramón Menéndez, 1988)
The Ballad of Gregorio Cortez (Robert M. Young, 1982)
The Book of Life (Jorge R. Gutiérrez, 2014)
The Casagrandes Movie (Miguel Puga, 2024)
The Counselor (Ridley Scott, 2013)
The Girl (David Riker, 2012)
The Rundown (Peter Berg, 2003)
They Are We (Emma Christopher, 2013)
Trade (Marco Kreuzpaintner, 2007)
Traffic (Steven Soderbergh, 2000)
Under the Same Moon / La misma luna (Patricia Riggen, 2008)
West Side Story (Robert Wise and Jerome Robbins, 1961)
We The Animals (Jeremiah Zagar, 2018)

FURTHER TV VIEWING

13 Reasons Why (2017–2020)
Altered Carbon (2018–2020)
Better Call Saul (2015–2022)
Black Mirror (2011–2019, 2023–)
Breaking Bad (2008–2013)
Charmed [reboot] (2018)
Chico and the Man (1974–1978)
CHiPs (1977–1983)
Claws (2017–2022)
Condo (1983)
Coyote (2021)
Cristela (2014–2015)
Dark Angel (2000–2002)
Diary of a Future President (2020–2021)
Doom Patrol (2019–2023)
East Los High (2013–2017)
El Tigre: The Adventures of Manny Rivera (2007–2008)
Euphoria (2019–)
Fantasy Island (1977–1984)
Fear the Walking Dead (2015–2023)
Fear the Walking Dead: Passage (2016)
From Dusk Till Dawn: The Series (Robert Rodriguez, 2014–2016)
Gentefied (2020–2021)
George Lopez (2002–2007)
Gordita Chronicles (2022)
Greetings from Tucson (2002–2003)
Griselda (2024)
Hightown (2020–2024)
House of Buggin' (1995)
I Love Lucy (1951–1957)
In Living Color (1990–1994)
Jane the Virgin (2014–2019)
John Leguizamo's Latin History for Morons (2018)
Julie and the Phantoms (2020)
La Reina del Sur (2011–2023)
Lopez (2016–2017)
Los Espookys (2019–2022)
Love, Victor (2020–2022)
L Word: Generation Q (2019–2023)
Mayans M.C. (2018–2023)
Miami Vice (1984–1989)
Modern Family (2009–2020)
Mr. Iglesias (2019–2020)
Narcos (2015–2017)
Never Have I Ever (2020–2023)

One Day at a Time [reboot] (2017–2020)
On My Block (2018–2021)
Orange Is the New Black (2013–2019)
Ozark (2017–2022)
Party of Five [reboot] (2020)
Penny Dreadful: City of Angels (2020)
Pose (2018–2021)
Primo (2023)
Queen of the South (2016–2021)
¿Qué Pasa, USA? (1977–1980)
Raising Dion (2019–2022)
Resurrection Blvd. (2000–2002)
Roswell, New Mexico (2019–2022)
Saturdays (2023)
Saved by the Bell (1989–1993)
Severance (2022–)
Shades of Blue (2016–2018)
Shameless season 10 (2020)
Sons of Anarchy (2008–2014)
Speedy Gonzales (1953–1955)
Stargirl (2020–2022)
Star Trek (1966–1969)
Station 19 (2018–2024)
Station Eleven (2021–2022)
Superman and Lois (2021–2024)
The Baker and the Beauty (2020)
The Book of Boba Fett (2021–2022)
The Boys (2019–2026)
The Expanding Universe of Ashley Garcia (2020)
The Falcon and the Winter Soldier (2021)
The Flash (2014–2023)
The High Chaparral (1967–1971)
The Last of Us (2023–)
The Mandalorian (2019–2023)
The Owl House (2020–2023)
The Proud Family: Louder and Prouder (2022–)
The Umbrella Academy season 2 (2020)
The Walking Dead (2010–2022)
Ugly Betty (2006–2010)
United We Fall (2020)
Vida (2018–2020)
Welcome Back, Kotter (1975–1979)
Wizards Beyond Waverly Place (2024–)
Wizards of Waverly Place (2007–2012)
Wonder Woman (1975–1979)

INDEX

ABOUT THE AUTHORS

FREDERICK LUIS ALDAMA (known as Professor Latinx) was born in Mexico City to a Guatemalan Irish American mother from Los Angeles and a Mexican father and raised in Northern California. He is an award-winning scholar, writer, and editor of over fifty books across fiction, nonfiction, comics, children's literature, and young adult literature. His creative works include the comic book *Pyroclast,* the young adult graphic fictions *Through Fences* and *Labyrinths Borne,* the novel *The Absolutely (Almost) True Adventures of Max Rodriguez,* and children's books such as *The Adventures of Chupacabra Charlie* and *Con Papá / With Papá.* Aldama has been recognized with numerous honors, including induction into the National Cartoonists Society, the Texas Institute of Letters, and The Ohio State University's Hall of Fame. He is the founder and director of the Latinx Pop Lab, serves on the board of the Academy of American Poets, and is editor-in-chief of both *Latinx Pop Magazine* and FlowerSong Press. He currently holds the Jacob & Frances Sanger Mossiker Chair in the Humanities at the University of Texas at Austin.

PETER MURRIETA was born and grew up in Tucson, Arizona, and is the descendant of the Mexican rebel and so-called bandit Joaquín Murrieta. He is an Emmy Award–winning screenwriter and producer, currently serving as deputy director of The Sidney Poitier New American Film School at Arizona State University. He is best known for his work as executive producer and head writer of the hit Disney Channel series *Wizards of Waverly Place,* which earned multiple Emmy Awards and continues to hold a special place in his creative legacy. Murrieta has also worked on popular TV shows such as *Cristela, One Day at a Time,* and *Lopez,* and received an Imagen Award for his work on *Mr. Iglesias.* His film credits include *Holidaze* (2006) and *Dealin' with Idiots* (2013). In addition to his TV and film work, Murrieta has written and published the comic book *Rafael Garcia: Henchman* and novel *Blood and Gold: The Legend of Joaquin Murrieta.*

